CYNTHIA HARTZELL

BREAKING THE CHAINS WITHIN

*Finding Inner Peace Through
the Wisdom of the Herd*

Proprietary Rights Statement

The concepts, exercises, and methods presented in *Breaking the Chains Within* reflect the original work and intellectual property of Cindy Hartzell. They are shared here for personal reflection and growth.

Reproduction, adaptation, or teaching of these methods in a professional or commercial capacity without written permission from the author is prohibited.

This material may form the foundation for future coaching programs, retreats, and professional certifications. For inquiries about participation or licensing, please contact email: cyahart@yahoo.com https://heartsoulhorsemanship.com

Table of Contents

The Call to Freedom

The room was quiet except for the faint rustle of paper and the steady rhythm of my breath. Sunlight streamed through the windows, illuminating dust particles that danced in the stillness. I had come to this writing retreat expecting to fill pages with ideas and insights, but instead, I found myself staring at the blank paper in front of me, as if the words I needed were locked away somewhere beyond my reach.

And then, it happened.

It wasn't a voice I heard with my ears, but a knowing—deep, resonant, and unmistakable. It came from within and beyond me all at once. It wasn't forceful, yet it demanded my attention with quiet certainty.

"You are living in a prison you cannot see."

I froze, pen hovering above the page. A chill crept up my spine. The words were stark and unyielding, like a truth I had been avoiding but always knew was there.

"You've built these walls yourself, brick by brick, from fear, doubt, and the stories you've carried since childhood. Stories you were taught to believe. But those walls don't protect you anymore—they trap you. It's time to let them go."

My heart raced as the weight of those words settled over me. In that moment, I could see it all so clearly—the ways I had confined myself, the patterns I clung to, and the beliefs that kept me small. On the outside, I had built a life of strength and achievement, but on the inside, I was caged, disconnected from the woman I knew I was meant to be.

Tears blurred my vision as I wrote the words pouring into my mind. The walls of my mental prison weren't made of stone or steel, but of fear: fear of failure, fear of rejection, fear of not being enough. I saw how they had kept me safe as a child, a protective mechanism against the chaos and pain of the world around me. But now, they were holding me back, keeping me from fully living the life I longed for.

"You have the power to break free," the voice continued. "The key is within you, waiting for you to use it. But you must burn the prison down and trust the path ahead."

Burn it down. The words felt both terrifying and exhilarating.

At that moment, I knew this wasn't just a metaphor. It was a call to action—a challenge to confront the fears and beliefs that had shaped me for so long. But how do you tear down walls that have become so familiar they feel like home?

As I stared out the window, my mind drifted to the horses in my life. Wild mustangs who had known captivity and freedom. Horses who had taught me lessons about trust, resilience, and connection. I realized that they had been my guides all along, reflecting back to me the truths I needed to see. Their ability to live in the present, free of shame or self-doubt, had always been a source of inspiration.

Their wisdom would be my roadmap, their presence my strength.

I took a deep breath and wrote one final sentence: "It's time to break the chains within."

The prison wasn't gone, but I could feel the first cracks forming. A glimmer of light filtered through, illuminating the path ahead. The journey wouldn't be easy, but for the first time, I felt ready. The horses had shown me that freedom wasn't a destination; it was a way of being, a choice I could make every day.

With a small smile, I picked up my pen and turned to the next blank page. It was time to write the rest of the story.

How to Use This Book

This book is more than a narrative; it is an invitation to embark on your own journey of growth, healing, and transformation. Each chapter weaves together stories, lessons, and reflections, offering insights into overcoming fear, reclaiming freedom, and living authentically. To help you integrate these lessons into your own life, I've included practical action steps at the end of each chapter.

Here's how you can get the most out of this book:

1. **Read with Intention**
   Approach each chapter with an open heart and mind. The stories and lessons are designed to inspire and challenge you. Allow yourself the space to reflect on how these ideas resonate with your own experiences.

2. **Engage with the Action Steps**
   The action steps at the end of each chapter are tools to help you put the concepts into practice. Take your time with them. Journaling, mindfulness exercises, and self-reflection can deepen your connection to the lessons and bring them into your daily life.

3. **Pause and Reflect**
   Don't rush through the book. Give yourself permission to pause, to reread sections that speak to you, and to let the ideas settle. Transformation happens over time, not in a single moment.

4. **Personalize the Journey**
   While the stories in this book are deeply personal, the lessons are universal. As you read, think about how the themes apply to

your own life. Use the action steps to explore your own patterns, beliefs, and relationships.

5. **Connect with the Lessons**

    This book draws heavily on lessons learned from working with horses and the wisdom they bring. If you have access to horses, consider how you can apply these ideas in your interactions with them. If not, the principles of trust, presence, and connection can still be applied to your relationships with others and yourself.

6. **Revisit Key Sections**

    As you grow and evolve, you may find new meaning in the lessons of this book. Keep it close, and revisit the chapters and action steps whenever you need guidance or inspiration.

7. **Share Your Journey**

    You are not alone in this process. Share your insights and experiences with others. Community and connection amplify growth, and your journey may inspire someone else to embark on their own.

CHAPTER 1

The Prison of the Mind

I sat in the quiet of the retreat center, a notebook open on my lap, its blank pages daring me to write. Outside, the wind whispered through the pines, carrying the scent of possibility. This was a space for reflection, a time to go inward and finally begin the book I'd always felt was inside me.

But instead, I sat in stillness, gripped by an unfamiliar emptiness. No words came—only questions.

Where are we supposed to go with this book? I wondered.

The voice that answered didn't sound like mine—or maybe it did, but from somewhere far deeper. Warm, steady, patient.

"To the deep beyond your rational awareness," it said.

I froze, my pen suspended in midair.

"You have experienced great shifts in the past six months, but you've had no time or space for processing. Your inner Higher Self has been silenced by the noise of your determination. You're missing the gentle sweetness of what you're doing... and who you are at the depth of your soul."

The words shimmered in my mind like threads of light. I set the pen down, breath shallow, an ache surfacing in my chest—a longing for something I couldn't name, only feel.

My life had always been about pushing forward. There was never time to pause, never space to reflect. There were goals to meet, clients to serve, horses to care for, and the never-ending demands of the ranch. I was always busy, always moving—driven by a force I thought was ambition, but now suspected was fear.

Fear of what? Fear of stopping. Fear of looking inward. Fear of being still long enough to hear the whispers of my own heart.

The voice returned, softer now, urging me to listen. *"Relax. Sit back and enjoy the journey. There is power in the pause—you teach it, you understand it, you know its great value. Now is the time to experience it."*

My shoulders sagged under the weight of my exhaustion. I felt so tired. My eyes wanted to close, my body wanted to collapse, yet my mind resisted. It clung to the familiar cycle of doing.

The voice grew firmer. *"Your nervous system desperately needs a reset. Stop trying to hold it all together. Surrender to this moment. Rest, at least for the next three days."*

That's when the image came—sudden, vivid: a prison. Not of stone or steel, but built from my own thoughts, beliefs, and fears. Barriers forged over years of survival, each brick a story or wound that had taken root.

Inside, I saw her—a woman radiant and beautiful, standing behind the bars. Her presence was magnetic, almost otherworldly. She stood tall, but her eyes carried the pain of someone who had endured confinement so long, she had forgotten what freedom felt like.

In the corner of the cell, a young girl crouched, arms wrapped tightly around her knees. Her eyes darted warily, but somewhere within them flickered a spark—hope, maybe, or curiosity.

I knew them both. The woman was my authentic self—the fullest expression of who I was meant to be. The child was my younger self, the innocent part of me locked away by years of shame, guilt, and fear. And the prison... that was my mind. Its walls were built from other people's stories that had become my own.

The voice spoke again. *"This is where you have been living. The prison of your mind. You are both the prisoner and the jailer. But the key to freedom is in your hands. You only need to open the door."*

Tears blurred my vision. How many years had I lived behind these walls, thinking they were here to protect me? How many times had I felt the urge to step out, only to be pulled back by fear—fear of failure, fear of success, fear of being seen, fear of shining too brightly and making others uncomfortable.

For a moment, my thoughts drifted to the horses. Their untamed beauty. The way they lived unburdened by the past, rooted in the present. I thought of Apache, the wild mustang who had come into my life years ago. His journey mirrored mine—a creature of the wild learning to trust again after a lifetime of fear.

Apache's mistrust was bone-deep. It took years—not weeks—to come close enough to touch him. But in that long, patient process, he became one of my greatest teachers. Apache showed me that trust is never taken—it's earned, moment by moment, with presence and consistency. He taught me patience, vulnerability, and the quiet courage it takes to open yourself to connection. Even now, he continues to hold up a mirror, reflecting truths about myself I might never have seen without him.

Maybe, I thought, *that's what I need to give myself.*

And then, as if conjured by the thought, a match appeared in my hand. Small, almost weightless—and yet, heavy with meaning. I knew what it symbolized: the courage to release the stories that had kept me confined. The choice to burn down the walls I once built for safety, but which had become my prison.

With a trembling hand, I struck the match. The flame leapt to life, golden and alive. I hesitated only a heartbeat, then tossed it toward the prison.

The fire roared—hungry, cleansing—devouring the bars and walls.

I turned.

I wasn't alone. Beside me, the child clasped my hand. On my other side, the radiant woman held the child's hand. Together we walked away from the burning prison.

On my left, Rocky moved in step with me, his steady presence grounding me. On the woman's right, RC walked with quiet dignity, his wisdom like a deep current beneath the surface. The five of us moved forward together, leaving the flames behind.

The voice came once more—not as instruction, but as a reminder. *"This is only the beginning."*

I picked up my pen. It felt heavier now, charged with meaning. The words came—not from my mind, but from somewhere deeper.

"She burst right open from her heart center into the world. Newborn perspectives, visions, sights, and sounds. Confusion and curiosity all at the same time. What is this world I am in? It seems so familiar, yet it is not the same. Who am I? This person I see looking back at me? Where are all the things I once held so dear to me?"

The words flowed like water. And I understood—this wasn't just a book. This was a journey. A healing. My chance to set myself free... and maybe help others do the same.

I could feel the prison walls inside me beginning to crumble.

Action Steps for Chapter 1: The Prison of the Mind

The first chapter explores the metaphorical prison of the mind, built from fear, guilt, shame, and unworthiness. It sets the stage for breaking free from limiting beliefs and taking the first step toward transformation. Here are practical steps to help you identify and begin dismantling your own inner prisons.

Belief: a thought that is imbued with emotions, that one believes to be true. A limiting belief is a thought that negatively impacts you.

1. Reflect on Your Inner Prison:

Take a quiet moment to reflect and write down the following:

- What beliefs, thoughts or fears make you feel trapped or stuck in your life?
- Where do you think these come from? Were they shaped by past experiences, relationships, or societal influences and expectations placed on them
- How do these thoughts or feelings hold you back from being your authentic self?

Example prompt: "If I didn't believe [insert limiting belief], how would my life be different?"

2. Identify Your Inner Guardrails:

The prison walls are held up by the stories we tell ourselves. Try this exercise to recognize those stories:

- Write down one recurring negative thought you have about yourself.
- Beneath it, write down evidence that disproves this thought. For example:
  - Negative thought: "I always fail."
  - Evidence: "I succeeded in [insert example]. Even when I failed, I learned something valuable."

3. Create a Releasing Ceremony:

Create a ceremony that will assist in letting go of one piece of your inner prison. This could be:

- Writing your limiting beliefs on paper and tearing them up.
- Meditating and visualizing the prison dissolving around you as you take deep, intentional breaths.
- Lighting a candle to symbolize burning away the weight of guilt, shame, or fear.

4. Presence Practice:

In this chapter, the journey begins with the realization that freedom starts with a single step. Practicing presence helps to ground yourself in the moment:

- Sit comfortably and close your eyes. Breathe deeply, focusing on breathing deeply into your belly area.
- As thoughts arise, label them without judgment ("that's fear," "that's doubt"), and imagine them passing like clouds in the sky.

5. Journal Your Breakthrough Moment:

Imagine you are standing in the doorway of your prison, ready to break free. Answer the following:

- What does freedom feel like to you?
- What is one small step you can take today to move closer to that freedom?
- Who or what supports you in this journey toward wholeness?

Invitation for Deeper Engagement:

Consider exploring how these practices align with your own transformational journey. If you're ready to take your next step with guidance, think about reaching out to mentors or exploring programs like mine that foster trust, freedom, and connection.

CHAPTER 2

Burning It Down

The vision of the prison stayed with me long after I put my pen down. It wasn't just an image—it was a feeling. The beautiful woman and the cautious child lingered in my mind, both unsettling and strangely grounding. They didn't say anything. They didn't need to. It felt like they were waiting. Waiting for me to do something, to take a step, to make the first move. But how? How was I supposed to free them when the walls of the prison felt so solid, so deeply rooted in my thoughts?

Those walls—they weren't just there to hold me back. They were there to keep me safe. At least, that's what I had always believed. And the guards? Oh, they were relentless. Doubt, shame, fear—they whispered in a steady chorus.

You'll fail.
They'll judge you.
You don't deserve freedom.

For years, I listened. Their voices felt like rules I had no choice but to follow. But now, for the first time, their words felt different—less like commands and more like distant echoes. As if they were fading.

The Moment of Clarity

Clarity often shows up when you least expect it. For me, it came one quiet evening while I was brushing Rocky. The training area was quiet, with only the gentle sounds of horses and the rustle of wildlife in the sagebrush. The rhythm of the brush was comforting, almost meditative. And then, out of nowhere, the voice returned.

"Burn it down."

I froze, the brush hovering mid-stroke. Burn what down? I wondered, though part of me already knew.

"The prison," the voice said. "You've lived there long enough. It's time to let it go."

The words hit like a spark, igniting something in me. I closed my eyes, and the image of the prison came back—the cold, gray walls, the shadows lurking in every corner. Each brick seemed to tell a story: fear of rejection, the need to be perfect, the belief that I wasn't enough. In the middle of it all stood the woman, calm and resolute. The child clung to her hand, her wide eyes darting between the walls and the open door. They were waiting for me.

The Fire Within

That night, I couldn't shake the vision. Sitting cross-legged in my meditation space, journal resting beside me, I closed my eyes and allowed the image to unfold. I saw myself standing at the entrance to the prison, the heavy iron door creaking open as if it had waited a lifetime for this moment.

The beautiful woman stepped out first, her gaze steady yet cautious. Her movements carried both strength and hesitation, as though she wasn't sure what freedom might feel like. Behind her came the child, her small hand gripping the woman's tightly. Together, we stood in the open air, the cool breeze brushing against our faces, carrying a sense of possibility—and fear.

Even as we stood outside those walls, free from the confines of the prison, I felt it—a heavy pull deep in my chest. Fear. It was a sensation I knew all too well, the kind I've seen reflected in a horse standing at the edge of danger. Like a horse at the threshold of a burning barn, its instincts torn between the safety of the familiar and the terrifying unknown, I too hesitated. The barn may be ablaze, the smoke suffocating, but to step away meant leaving behind what had once felt safe, even if that safety was an illusion.

That pull—the pull of the familiar—was overwhelming. The prison, for all its darkness, had been predictable. Its walls defined the edges of my world, providing a sense of control. Letting it go meant stepping into a vast unknown where there were no barriers to lean on, no walls to hide behind.

I could feel the hesitation ripple through the beautiful woman standing beside me. She paused, her hand tightening protectively around the child's. The child looked up, her wide eyes meeting mine, reflecting a mix of fear and something else—something quieter but no less powerful: hope.

The voice of my Higher Self spoke clearly, cutting through the haze of doubt. It was steady, firm, and kind.

"You don't need this anymore," it said. "It's time to let it go."

Lighting the Match

In the stillness of my meditation, a match appeared in my hand. Small and nearly weightless, it seemed impossible that something so fragile could hold such power. Yet, as the flame flickered to life, its golden light cast shadows against the walls of the prison. My hand trembled as I held it, the significance of what I was about to do pressing heavily on my heart.

And then, with a deep breath, I threw it.

The fire caught instantly, consuming the walls and spreading with a ferocity I hadn't expected. Flames roared as they devoured the bricks, reducing them to ash. The guards' voices—the whispers of fear and doubt that had controlled me for so long—faded into silence, swallowed by the crackling inferno. The prison was gone, nothing left but smoke curling into the sky and embers glowing faintly in the dark.

As the fire burned, an unexpected wave of grief washed over me. It caught me off guard, though perhaps it shouldn't have. Those walls had been my shelter for so long, the only home I'd known. Even as they crumbled, I felt the ache of their loss. I mourned the comfort of their familiarity, even as I embraced the relief of their destruction.

The child looked up at me, her voice soft but steady.

"What now?"

The beautiful woman turned to me, her presence calm and sure. She held the answer I was just beginning to understand.

"Now," she said, "we begin."

Stepping Into Freedom

The next morning, I woke up with a sense of clarity I hadn't felt in years. Burning down the prison had been a turning point, a moment of release. But I knew it was only the beginning. Destroying the walls was one thing; learning how to live without them was another.

Doubt tried to creep back in as I sat with my journal, the blank page staring up at me.

What if you can't do it? What if you fail?

But this time, I didn't let the whispers take root. I placed a hand over my heart, closed my eyes, and took a deep breath. The prison was gone. The fear was still there, but it no longer had the power to control me.

Later that day, I was visiting with Rocky. He stood grazing peacefully, his coat gleaming in the sunlight. Watching him, I marveled at his ability to settle into this new place, to trust that he was safe.

When Rocky first arrived, his life had been turned upside down. Everything familiar—his home, his people, his routine—was gone. He had been wary, unsure, guarded, yet there was an air of quiet confidence about him.

From the start, we shared a bond that felt as though it had existed long before we met, and it was that connection that gave him the courage to begin trusting me and his new home. Still, he remained extremely aware of his surroundings, needing plenty of moments to pause and take in the unfamiliar sights, sounds, smells, and the herd.

It struck me how similar his journey was to my own. Like me, he had been uprooted from the familiar and thrown into the unknown. Like me, he had resisted, clinging to old patterns of fear and self-protection. And like me, his freedom had come not from running away, but from learning to trust.

Learning to Trust

Earning Rocky's trust had taken time. I had to show him, over and over, that he was safe, that he had a voice, that his boundaries mattered. I didn't rush him or push him; I simply showed up, consistently and patiently. Slowly, he began to relax. Slowly, he began to trust me.

Standing there, watching him graze, I realized I needed to extend the same patience to myself. Just as Rocky had needed space to grieve what he had lost and to trust what was new, I needed to offer myself that same grace.

Freedom isn't something that happens all at once. It's earned, moment by moment, as we find the courage to trust what lies ahead.

That night, I sat down to write again. The words flowed easily, as if they had been waiting for this moment.

"This book is my story," I wrote, "but it's also yours. It's about breaking free from the prisons we build in our minds, about burning down the walls of fear and shame, and stepping into the light of our true selves. It's about learning to trust, to pause, and to listen to the voice of our Higher Self. It's about freedom."

As I closed my journal, I felt a quiet certainty settle over me. The prison was gone, and for the first time in a long time, I felt truly free.

Action Steps for Chapter 2: Recognizing the Prison of the Mind

The journey of freedom begins with awareness—acknowledging the thoughts, beliefs, and patterns that keep you confined. In this chapter, we explored the concept of the "prison of the mind," those self-imposed limitations that stem from fear, shame, guilt, and unworthiness. These steps will help you identify your own "prison walls" and begin dismantling them.

1. Identify Your Limiting Beliefs

Take a moment to reflect on the areas of your life where you feel stuck or held back. Use the prompts below to uncover the limiting beliefs that may be shaping your thoughts and behaviors:

- What do I believe about myself that might not be true?
- What do I tell myself about what I can or cannot do?
- What fears are stopping me from taking action?

Write down at least three beliefs that you recognize as limiting. For example:

- "I'll never be good enough."
- "If I speak up, I'll be judged."
- "I can't succeed because I've failed before."

2. Reframe a Limiting Belief

Choose one of the beliefs you've identified and practice reframing it into an empowering belief. For instance:

- Limiting belief: "I'm not good enough."
- Reframed belief: "I am worthy, and I'm learning and growing every day."

Write down your new belief and repeat it to yourself daily, especially when you notice the old belief surfacing. Each day, close your eyes, quiet your mind through your breathing, and from your heart state your new belief from the quiet space within your heart.

3. Create Space for Self-Compassion

Self-compassion is a powerful tool for breaking free from shame and guilt. Spend 5–10 minutes in quiet reflection. Begin by placing a hand over your heart and taking 4 deep breaths down into your power center.

Your power center is 2–3' below your belly button and deep in the center of your pelvic bowl. Once there, begin repeating a compassionate affirmation such as:

- "I am doing my best, and that is enough."
- "I forgive myself for past mistakes."
- "I am worthy of love and understanding."

Notice how it feels to speak kindly to yourself. If resistance arises, acknowledge it without judgment and gently continue.

4. Observe the "Prison Walls" in Action

Throughout the next week, pay attention to moments when you feel fear, self-doubt, or resistance. When they arise:

1. Pause and take 4 deep breaths into your power center.
2. Ask yourself: *Is this thought or feeling coming from my "prison walls"?*
3. If so, remind yourself: *I have the power to choose a different story.*

Jot down these observations in a journal. Awareness is the first step to change.

5. Visualize Your Freedom

Create 5–10 minutes in your day to find a quiet place and allow your body and mind to rest. Close your eyes, take 4–6 deep breaths into your power center, allowing you to become still and grounded in the present moment. Imagine stepping outside the walls of your "prison." Picture yourself walking into a wide, open space filled with possibility. Ask yourself:

- What does freedom look like for me?
- What would I do if I truly believed I was enough?

Write about this vision in your journal, letting it inspire your next steps.

Closing Reminder

Recognizing the prison of the mind is a brave and powerful step. As you explore these action steps, know that transformation is a journey—one that begins with small, intentional choices to see yourself with compassion and to believe in the possibility of freedom.

CHAPTER 3

Trust Begins at the Heart

Rocky's arrival at the ranch marked the beginning of a journey neither of us could have anticipated. He had come to me carrying the weight of displacement, uncertainty, and fear. I, too, was stepping into unfamiliar territory, navigating the early days of my own transformation. Together, we would learn what it meant to build trust—not as something granted, but as something earned through time, patience, and understanding.

When I first stood by his trailer, coaxing him to step into his new life, his hesitation was palpable. His body shifted nervously, his ears flicking back and forth, listening for cues that would tell him if this was safe or if danger was looming. His hooves were rooted to the trailer floor, as if leaving it would sever his last tie to the familiar.

"It's okay," I whispered, keeping my voice steady, my movements slow. "You're safe now."

I could feel his fear as if it were my own. Horses have a way of sharing their emotions, bypassing the walls we humans put up. They make you feel things you didn't even know you were carrying. In that moment, I understood that the safety I was offering Rocky wasn't just for him—it was for me, too.

Building trust with Rocky wasn't easy. There were days when he stood quietly, allowing me to approach, his body relaxed and his eyes soft. But there were also days when he seemed distant, withdrawing into himself as if caught in memories of the life he'd left behind. It was as though he were grieving—missing his old home, his herd, the familiar rhythm of his days. Those moments, when his longing seemed to weigh heavier than his curiosity, tested me the most. They reminded me that trust isn't just about connection—it's about giving space for the heart to process and heal.

I had learned that you can't force trust, especially with a horse like Rocky. He wasn't going to give me his confidence just because I wanted it. He needed proof—consistency, presence, and a willingness to meet him where he was.

A few weeks after he arrived, I was at one of the ranches where I teach horsemanship lessons and had brought Rocky along. We were in the arena with a student and her horses. After riding, I dismounted, secured his reins over the saddle horn, and stepped away to assist my student. I hadn't gone far when I noticed movement behind me. Turning, I saw Rocky following me, his head low, his gaze soft and relaxed. I continued walking, weaving around the arena, and he stayed with me, mirroring each step as though we were connected by an invisible thread. It was in that moment I knew—he had chosen me as his partner.

That day, I realized how much I had been holding my own breath, waiting for him to trust me. His simple act of following me was like a mirror, reflecting back my own need to trust—not just him, but myself. In that quiet exchange, I felt the first flicker of something I hadn't realized I was seeking: hope.

Over time, as Rocky began to let go of his fear, I saw pieces of myself reflected in his journey. His hesitations mirrored my own struggles with stepping into the unknown. His small acts of bravery reminded me of my own tentative steps toward freedom.

I thought back to a time when I sat in the pasture with RC, my beloved palomino. After the accident, when I lost my finger, the disconnect between us was overwhelming. I avoided him for weeks, unsure of how to rebuild what we had lost.

The space between us felt hollow, heavy with everything we'd lost. What once connected us was gone, leaving only confusion, loneliness, and sadness in its place. Yet, despite the weight of it all, I finally found the courage to sit still in his presence.

As the silence settled around us, my head dropped, and the tears came—uncontrollable and endless. I didn't try to hide them this time. He walked over to me, his own head low, tears streaming down his face. Our separate griefs seemed to meet in the space between us, heavy but unspoken. When I finally looked up, his pain was unmistakable, mirroring my own. Without a word, we sat together—two broken souls bound by sorrow, finding solace in the quiet presence of one another.

That moment became a quiet turning point—not just in our fragile relationship, but in my understanding of what it meant to heal. Healing wasn't something to be forced or rushed. It was this: the courage to sit with the pain, to let the tears come, and to trust in the unspoken connection that grew naturally between us. For the first time in a long while, I felt the faint stirrings of hope—small, but undeniable.

There was a purity in my interactions with Rocky that mirrored those early days of reconnection with RC. Horses don't care about the stories you tell yourself or the facades you put up. They respond to energy, to presence, to the truth of who you are in that moment.

Being with Rocky reminded me that trust isn't something you build all at once. It's a quiet, patient process—a series of small, imperfect moments that add up over time. It's about showing up, even when it feels like nothing is changing. And it's about finding meaning in the little milestones: the first time he didn't shy away when I approached, the first time he lingered close without hesitation, the first time he let out a soft breath and chose to stay. But Rocky wasn't the only one who had taught me these lessons. Every horse who had come into my life carried their own challenges and gifts. Each had shown me something different about myself—my patience, my fears, my capacity for connection.

Apache, the wild mustang who had taken years to trust me enough to allow a single touch, had been one of my most humbling teachers. His fear and mistrust were profound, and yet his resilience was even greater. Through Apache, I learned that trust can't be rushed—it requires a deep respect for the other's boundaries and a willingness to slow down.

Troubadour, the palomino rescued from a kill pen, came into my life at a time when I was grieving the limitations RC's condition had placed on us. Troubadour's guarded demeanor reminded me of the power of patience and the beauty of rediscovering connection, not as a replacement but as a new chapter in my journey.

And Mira, the spirited filly who seemed to dance through life with endless curiosity, had taught me to embrace the unknown with wonder instead of hesitation. Her fearlessness was a reflection of what I aspired to be—a reminder that even in unfamiliar territory, there is beauty in exploration.

Each horse had been a reflection of a part of me. The ones who were skittish and mistrusting showed me my own struggles with vulnerability. The ones who pushed boundaries and tested limits held a mirror to my own need for growth and structure. And the ones who surrendered to the moment, who leaned into connection, reminded me of what it felt like to be fully present and open.

That day with Rocky, as I walked back to the house, I felt a quiet sense of gratitude for all the lessons these horses had brought into my life. They had taught me far more than I could ever teach them. They had shown me how to trust, how to listen, how to be patient. They had guided me out of my own prison, step by step, simply by being themselves.

I thought of the journey still ahead, both for me and for the horses I worked with. There would be setbacks and challenges, moments of frustration, and days when progress felt slow or nonexistent. But there would also be breakthroughs, quiet triumphs, and the kind of connection that couldn't be put into words. The path forward wasn't about reaching some final destination—it was about being present for each step, about honoring the process, both theirs and mine.

Later that evening, as I sat with my journal, I reflected on the gifts each horse had brought into my life. Each was a teacher, a mirror, and a companion on this path of transformation. And as I thought about all they had given me, I realized that they hadn't just taught me how to work with them—they had taught me how to work with myself.

Action Steps for Chapter 3: Trust Begins at the Heart

Building trust is a foundational element in relationships, whether with others, ourselves, or even animals like Apache. The lessons from this chapter highlight the importance of presence, patience, and mutual respect in fostering connection. Here are actionable steps to help you integrate these lessons into your own journey of trust-building.

1. Practice Quiet Presence

Horses respond to the energy we bring into their space, and so do people and even our inner selves. To begin building trust, start by cultivating a sense of quiet presence.

- **Exercise:**
  - Find a quiet space where you won't be disturbed. Sit still and simply observe your surroundings. Notice the sights, sounds, and sensations without judgment.
  - Breathe deeply, focusing on calming your energy. Imagine radiating calm and safety to yourself and out and around you like a bubble or a snow globe.

- **Why It Helps:**
  - This practice grounds you in the present moment and helps you bring a calming presence to yourself and interactions with others.

2. Listen Without an Agenda

Trust grows when others feel heard and respected. This applies to human relationships, your inner dialogue, and interactions with animals.

- **Exercise:**
  - Choose one interaction each day to focus solely on listening. Whether it's with a friend, family member, or your own inner thoughts, set aside your desire to respond or fix.
  - Pay attention to body language, tone, and emotions. What is being communicated beyond the words?

- **Why It Helps:**
  - Active listening creates space for connection and understanding. It's an essential step in building trust.

3. Celebrate Small Victories

As this chapter illustrates, trust is built incrementally—through the small steps each horse and I took together. Acknowledge progress, no matter how small, in your own journey or in your relationships.

- **Exercise:**
  - Keep a journal and write down one small victory each day. It could be anything from feeling calmer in a challenging situation to noticing someone else's effort to connect with you.
  - Reflect on why this moment mattered and how it contributes to building trust.

- **Why It Helps:**
  - Focusing on small wins helps you stay motivated and reinforces positive behavior patterns.

4. Respect Boundaries

Rocky's journey showed the importance of honoring boundaries as part of trust-building. This applies to both external relationships and your own internal needs.

- **Exercise:**
  - Identify one boundary that feels important to you, whether it's taking time for self-care, saying no to an obligation, or honoring someone else's need for space.
  - Practice upholding or respecting this boundary without guilt or frustration.

- **Why It Helps:**
  - Boundaries create a safe environment for trust to grow. They signal mutual respect and understanding.

5. Mirror Your Energy

Just as horses mirror our energy, relationships and situations often reflect what we bring into them. Use this concept to explore how your internal state influences your external experiences.

- **Exercise:**
  - The next time you face a challenging interaction, pause and check in with yourself. Are you bringing tension, impatience, or calmness into the situation?
  - Adjust your energy intentionally. If you're feeling rushed, slow down. If you're tense, take a deep breath and soften your body language.

- **Why It Helps:**
  Shifting your energy can change the dynamic of an interaction and pave the way for deeper connection and trust.

6. Reflect on Your Teachers

The chapter emphasizes how each horse acted as a teacher, reflecting a part of my own journey. Apply this concept by identifying who or what has been a teacher in your life.

- **Exercise:**
  - Write a list of people, experiences, or even animals that have taught you important lessons.
  - Reflect on what you learned from each and how those lessons have shaped you.

- **Why It Helps:**
  - Recognizing your teachers fosters gratitude and helps you see growth opportunities in every experience.

7. Be Patient with the Process

Trust-building, whether with yourself or others, is a gradual process. Accept that it will have ups and downs.

- **Exercise:**
  - The next time you feel frustrated with slow progress, remind yourself of Rocky's story. Repeat the mantra: "Trust is a dance, not a race."
  - Focus on showing up consistently, even when progress feels small.

- **Why It Helps:**
  - Patience allows trust to develop naturally and strengthens your resilience during setbacks.

Reflective Journal Prompts

To deepen your understanding and application of this chapter, consider the following questions:

1. Where in my life am I seeking to build trust? How can I show up consistently for that process?
2. What small victories can I celebrate today that reflect growth in trust or connection?
3. How do my own energy and emotions influence my relationships and interactions?

By integrating these steps into your daily life, you'll not only deepen your understanding of trust but also create a foundation for stronger connections—both with others and within yourself.

CHAPTER 4

The Pattern of Fear

The sensation came without warning—a tightening in my chest, a rush of heat to my face, a familiar knot of anxiety in my stomach. I was brushing Rocky when it hit me, the flood of thoughts I couldn't stop. *Am I doing enough? Am I getting it right? What if I'm failing him?*

Rocky glanced back, sensing the shift in my energy, his grazing halted as he turned to meet my gaze, his dark eyes wide and questioning. I froze, with brush in hand, and took a long breath, trying to calm the swirl of doubt in my mind. *This isn't about him,* I realized. *It's about me.*

Fear had always been my shadow. It lingered in the background, a constant hum beneath the surface of my thoughts. Sometimes it was quiet, almost imperceptible. Other times, it roared to life, wrapping itself around me like a storm I couldn't escape. Over the years, I had learned to live with it, to push through it, to keep going even when it threatened to overwhelm me. But now, standing next to Rocky, I realized how much power it still held.

The voice of my Higher Self broke through the noise, steady and clear. "This is the pattern," it said. "Fear isn't your prison anymore, but it still stands at the edge of your freedom. It no longer confines you, but it tries to keep you from moving forward."

I closed my eyes, letting the truth of those words sink in. The fear wasn't just about Rocky, or the horses, or my work. It was the story I had been telling myself my entire life: You're not enough. You're not worthy.

You'll never succeed. It was a script I had learned as a child, one that had shaped my thoughts, my actions, and my identity.

The pattern wasn't new. I could trace its roots back to my earliest memories—the moments when I had been scolded for being too loud, too curious, too much. The times when I had brought home an injured animal, my heart full of hope, only to be met with anger and rejection. The lessons I had learned: Don't stand out. Don't shine too brightly. Don't trust your instincts.

Those messages had planted seeds in my mind, seeds that grew into the tangled vines of doubt and fear that now wrapped around me. They were the reason I second-guessed myself, the reason I held back, the reason I struggled to fully embody my dreams.

But just as the horses had taught me, patterns could be broken. I had seen it happen time and again—horses who arrived at my ranch skittish and afraid, their bodies tense with the memory of past traumas. With patience, trust, and consistency, they learned to relax, to let go, to trust. If they could do it, so could I.

I thought back to Apache, the mustang whose fear ran so deep it had taken years for him to trust me enough to allow a single touch. When he first came into my life, I spent hours sitting outside his pen, doing nothing but being present. Slowly, he began to let me get closer, step by step. He taught me that fear wasn't something you could force away; it had to be met with patience and understanding. Trust was earned, moment by moment, through consistency and care.

That afternoon, I sat by the fence and watched the herd grazing. Rocky stood a little apart, his head low, his tail swishing lazily against the flies. His striking dun-and-white pinto coat gleamed in the sunlight, his thick mane rippling slightly in the breeze—a testament to his Gypsy Vanner heritage, blended with the athletic build of his Quarter Horse lineage. He had only been with me for a few weeks, but the changes in him were already evident. His body was softer, his movements less guarded. He had started to play with the other horses, testing the waters of belonging and connection.

I thought about the process we had gone through together, the small steps that had led to this point. I had started by giving him space, letting him come to me on his own terms. I had shown him that he had a voice, that his boundaries would be respected. Slowly, he had begun to trust me, to believe that he was safe.

Dakota, the matriarch of our herd, had been instrumental in Rocky's journey. Her calm, steady energy anchored the herd, providing a sense of safety and stability. She had a way of observing the world with a quiet confidence, stepping in to guide only when necessary. Watching her approach Rocky, I saw the embodiment of the leader I aspired to be— not forceful or demanding, but grounded, patient, and deeply intuitive.

She approached him slowly, her movements deliberate, her energy calm. She didn't demand his trust; she earned it through her presence and consistency. *This is who I want to be,* I thought. *Not just for the horses, but for myself.*

As I watched Rocky, my attention turned to Gino, a horse who had come into my life broken by years of abandonment and rejection. He, too, carried the weight of fear, rooted in the belief that he was unwanted. It took months to break through his walls, but when he finally began to trust me, his transformation was nothing short of miraculous. Gino taught me that trust begins not with the other, but with ourselves. It's about finding the courage to believe in the goodness within and letting it guide us.

The voice of my Higher Self returned, pulling me back to the present. "Fear is the pattern," it said again. "But it's also the key. When you face it, when you walk through it, you'll find freedom on the other side."

I nodded; my gaze fixed on Gino as he lifted his head to look at me. His ears pricked forward, his eyes soft and curious. He had faced his own fears and came out stronger on the other side. I could do the same.

That evening, I wrote in my journal, the words pouring out of me like a confession.

"Fear has been my constant companion, my shadow, my jailer. It has kept me small, kept me safe, kept me from fully stepping into my purpose. But I'm beginning to see it for what it is—a pattern, a story, a lie. I'm ready to let it go. I'm ready to step out of prison and into freedom. I'm ready to trust myself."

As I closed the journal, a sense of calm washed over me. The fear wasn't gone—it would likely never disappear completely—but it no longer felt insurmountable. I had tools now, lessons learned from the horses and from my own journey. I had a vision of the beautiful woman and the inner child walking into freedom. And I had hope.

In the days that followed, I began to notice the pattern more clearly. Every time fear surfaced, I would pause, take several deep breaths, and remind myself that I was safe. I treated myself the way I treated the horses—with patience, kindness, and trust. And slowly, I began to see the change.

Fear wasn't the enemy. It was the teacher, the guide, the reminder that I was on the edge of something new. And for the first time, I felt ready to step into it.

Action Steps for Chapter 4: The Pattern of Fear

This chapter delves into the powerful realization that fear is not the enemy but a guide—a pattern that, when understood, can be transformed into an opportunity for growth. The following action steps will help you identify, confront, and begin to reshape your relationship with fear, inspired by the lessons shared in this chapter.

1. Identify Your Fear Patterns

Fear often manifests as a recurring pattern in our thoughts and behaviors. The first step to transformation is recognizing these patterns.

- **Exercise:**
  - Take 10 minutes to reflect and journal on a recent moment when fear surfaced. What triggered it? How did it show up in your body? How did you react?
  - Look for recurring themes or stories you tell yourself (e.g., "I'm not good enough," "I'll never succeed"). Write them down.

- **Why It Helps:**
  - Identifying and becoming aware of your fear patterns helps you see them as stories rather than truths, giving you the power to change them.

2. Pause and Breathe

When fear arises, it's natural to react instinctively. Instead, practice pausing and grounding yourself in the moment.

- **Exercise:**
  - When you notice fear creeping in, stop what you're doing.
  - Take four slow, deep breaths, inhaling for a count of four, holding for a count of two, and exhaling for a count of six. Focus on your breath, letting it anchor you in the present.

- **Why It Helps:**
  - This technique calms your nervous system and creates space to respond intentionally rather than react out of fear.

3. Reframe Fear as a Teacher

Fear often signals that you're stepping into new territory. Instead of resisting it, approach it with curiosity.

- **Exercise:**
  - The next time you feel fear, ask yourself: What is this fear trying to teach me? What opportunity or growth might lie on the other side of it?
  - Write down your answers in a journal to reflect on later. Be sure to come back and take the time to reflect and even do more journaling about the experience.

- **Why It Helps:**
  - Reframing fear as a teacher shifts your mindset from avoidance to empowerment, helping you see fear as a guide rather than a barrier.

4. Practice Small Acts of Trust

Building trust with yourself, as with others, happens through consistent, small actions over time.

- **Exercise:**
  - Choose one small step each day that requires you to face a fear or discomfort (e.g., having a difficult conversation, trying something new, or allowing yourself to rest without guilt).
  - Celebrate each step, no matter how small, as a victory toward building self-trust.

- **Why It Helps:**
  - Consistently showing up for yourself builds confidence and reinforces the belief that you can handle challenges.

5. Embrace the Power of Presence

As seen with Rocky and the horses, presence is a powerful antidote to fear. Staying present allows you to meet fear with calm and clarity.

- **Exercise:**
  - Spend five minutes each day in a mindfulness practice, such as observing your surroundings, meditating, or simply sitting quietly.
  - If your mind wanders to fears or doubts, gently bring it back to the present moment by focusing on your breath or a simple mantra like, "I am here. I am safe."

- **Why It Helps:**
  - Being present helps you step out of the stories fear tells and into the reality of the moment, where possibilities exist.

6. Journal to Uncover the Roots of Fear

Fear is often rooted in past experiences or conditioning. Journaling can help uncover and release these origins.

- **Exercise:**
  - Set aside time to write about a fear you're experiencing. Ask yourself: When did I first feel this fear? What messages or beliefs might have created it? How is it serving or protecting me now?
  - Reflect on how you might begin to rewrite this narrative.

- **Why It Helps:**
  - o Understanding the roots of your fear gives you insight into how it's shaped your patterns and how you can begin to change them.

7. Create a Supportive Environment

Just as Rocky's transformation required a calm, consistent environment, your growth benefits from external support.

- **Exercise:**
  - o Surround yourself with people, practices, and spaces that support your journey. This might mean spending time with trusted friends, creating a peaceful home environment, or working with a mentor or coach.
  - o Set boundaries with anything that exacerbates your fear or drains your energy.

- **Why It Helps:**
  - o A supportive environment fosters safety and growth, making it easier to face and transform fear.

Reflective Journal Prompts

1. What patterns of fear do I notice in my life, and how have they shaped my choices?
2. How can I show myself patience and understanding, as I would with a horse like Rocky or Apache?
3. What small steps can I take today to face a fear and build trust in myself?

By engaging with these steps, you'll begin to see fear not as a limitation but as an opportunity—a chance to deepen your trust in yourself, connect with your inner strength, and step boldly into the unknown.

CHAPTER 5

Lessons from the Mustangs

The mustangs were unlike any other horses I had worked with. There was a wildness in them, a rawness that felt untamed and sacred. Their energy wasn't dulled by domestication; it was sharp, alive, and unyielding. These were creatures of instinct and survival, shaped by the open plains and the harsh realities of the wild.

As I watched them from the dirt road on my first day at the sanctuary, I felt both awe and curiosity. I couldn't have known then how much they would teach me—not just about themselves, but about the wildness and freedom I was learning to reclaim within myself.

These were the Virginia Range mustangs, once wild and free, roaming the rugged landscapes of Nevada. Their lives had been disrupted by the rapid encroachment of human development. They weren't federally protected, so when their land was sold off, they became the property of the Nevada Department of Agriculture. Classified as "feral," they were rounded up and sent to auction. Their fate could have been devastating, but a group of passionate women—people who had known many of these horses since birth—stepped in, rescuing them just in time.

Once at the sanctuary, I joined the group of volunteers working to care for the horses. It was a crisp winter morning, the air biting at my face as I bundled up in layers before heading out on foot to meet them. Standing by the pasture, I watched a band of about 25 mustangs eating hay. Their movements were mesmerizing—each flick of an ear, swish of a tail, or shuffle of hooves told a story. These were horses adjusting to their new reality, finding their footing after everything they had known was taken from them. It mirrored my own journey in ways I didn't yet fully understand.

A Sacred Encounter

Each mustang seemed to carry its own story, its own lesson. Among them, one horse stood out—a dark bay mare who would become one of my greatest teachers.

Looking back now, it's hard to believe how much time has passed since that first encounter with her at the sanctuary. I remember that day vividly, as though it happened yesterday. The group of us had followed the band of mustangs toward the open pasture, carrying bags of carrots to offer as an olive branch. But something in me urged caution, urging me to hang back and observe from a distance.

I climbed a ridge, seeking a better view of the horses grazing below, when I saw her. She was solid and dark, her coat shimmering in the sunlight, moving with quiet authority alongside two others. Even then, she stood apart—not just in appearance, but in energy. I watched as our paths converged, both of us drawn to the same spot. I stopped, rooted to the ground, and let her make the next move.

Her eyes met mine, piercing through the barriers I didn't even realize I was holding. Slowly, she approached, breathing me in deeply before presenting her neck and shoulder. I reached out tentatively, marveling at the softness of her coat, as if her very presence had been a gift meant only for me. When another horse tried to approach, she pinned her ears and drove him off, circling back as though to claim me.

That day, DreamCatcher chose me, and though it would be months before she came home, the connection was undeniable. When she finally joined our herd in 2013, becoming the first mustang I adopted, I knew our journey was just beginning.

DreamCatcher has carried those lessons forward in her own way, becoming a teacher during the women's retreats we host at the ranch. She has a way of inviting women to reconnect with their inner Goddess Warrior, guiding them to find strength in their vulnerability and power in their presence.

Reflecting on those early days, I see now how the mustangs, each in their own time, have brought me exactly what I needed—whether it was the strength to trust, the courage to lead, or the wisdom to embrace the moment. DreamCatcher's whisper, "I will someday go home with you," was more than a promise; it was the beginning of a journey that continues to shape my life and the lives of those who meet her.

Lessons in Leadership and Trust

While DreamCatcher had chosen me on that first day, the lessons I would learn from the mustangs didn't stop there. Apache's story unfolded months later, but his impact was just as profound.

It was a late spring morning, and I had arrived at the sanctuary eager to spend time with DreamCatcher before heading to Reno for a volunteer shift with the mustang non-profit. The pastures stretched out before me, dotted with grazing bands of horses, their winter coats clinging to them despite the season's change.

As I made my way through the pasture, searching for DreamCatcher, a roan-colored mustang caught my eye. He darted between bands, pursued relentlessly by a commanding bay horse with a snaking head and ears pinned back in aggression. The roan moved with caution, trailing me at a safe distance, as though searching for safety.

When I finally found DreamCatcher near the fence with a sorrel mare, my relief was short-lived. The same bay horse appeared again, driving away other horses with swift precision. His energy was undeniable—focused and intense, his dominance palpable. As he turned his attention toward DreamCatcher, my instinct took over.

I stepped between them, blocking him from reaching her. He veered off but circled back moments later, his intent clear. DreamCatcher remained perfectly still, her trust in me grounding both of us. As he approached again, I raised my glove and blocked him with a firm but gentle motion. To my surprise, he reared slightly, spun, and bolted, leaving DreamCatcher and me standing together, both a little stunned by what had just unfolded.

That moment was a turning point for both of us. DreamCatcher had placed her trust in me, and I had risen to the challenge. It was on that day that I gave the bay horse his name: Apache.

In 2014, Apache joined our herd at the ranch, bringing his indomitable spirit into our daily lives. Even now, his wild instincts remain a constant inner battle, caught between his natural need for freedom and his growing trust in me. Each interaction with him reminds me of the delicate balance between connection and independence, and the patience it takes to honor his journey.

Reflecting on Apache's story now, I see how his lessons echoed those of DreamCatcher and Dakota. Apache embodied the strength and determination to follow his wild instincts, challenging me to honor both his nature and my own. DreamCatcher, from the first day we met, showed me how some connections are simply meant to be—intuitive, magical, and undeniable. Dakota, the matriarch of my current herd, continues to teach me the grace and quiet wisdom of steady leadership. Each of these mustangs has shaped my understanding of trust, connection, and the courage it takes to show up fully.

Final Reflection

For the first time in a long time, I felt ready to trust the process. DreamCatcher had shown me the power of quiet connection, Apache challenged me to embrace leadership and boundaries, and Dakota reminded me of the grace found in quiet strength.

The mustangs had shown me a new way of being—one that didn't require walls or defenses, one that embraced vulnerability as a pathway to connection. Their wildness wasn't something to tame; it was something to honor, a reminder of the untamed beauty within all of us.

They were more than horses—they were reflections of the freedom I was learning to claim for myself.

Action Steps for Chapter 5: Lessons from the Mustangs

In Chapter 5, we explored the profound lessons that mustangs teach us about trust, connection, and presence. These wild, resilient horses embody the essence of authenticity and remind us of the importance of patience and respect in building relationships. These action steps will help you integrate the wisdom of the mustangs into your life, enhancing your ability to connect authentically with both yourself and others.

1. Observe Without Judgment

Mustangs teach us the power of observation. Practice observing situations and relationships in your life without immediately assigning judgment:

- Find a quiet moment to observe someone you care about or your own thoughts and emotions.

- Ask yourself: *What do I notice about their (or my) energy, body language, or behavior? What might they (or I) be trying to communicate?*
- Resist the urge to react immediately. Instead, allow the observation to guide your understanding.

2. Practice Patience

Building trust, whether with a mustang or in human relationships, requires time and consistency:

- Identify a relationship or situation where trust is being built or repaired.
- Commit to small, consistent actions that demonstrate your reliability, such as being present, listening attentively, or following through on promises.
- Remind yourself that trust is a journey, not a destination.

3. Honor Boundaries

Mustangs thrive when their boundaries are respected. Apply this principle to your interactions:

- Reflect on where you might need to set or honor boundaries in your life.
- Practice saying no to things that don't align with your values or well-being, and respect when others do the same.
- Remember that boundaries create the foundation for healthy, respectful relationships.

4. Be Present in the Moment

Mustangs live fully in the present, responding to what is happening here and now. Practice cultivating presence:

- Spend 10 minutes each day focusing entirely on your surroundings. What do you see, hear, feel, and smell?
- When interacting with someone, give them your full attention. Put away distractions like phones and truly listen to what they are saying.
- Notice how being present changes the quality of your interactions.

5. Build Trust Through Consistency

Mustangs learn to trust through repeated, predictable actions that make them feel safe. Apply this principle in your own life:

- Choose one small action to perform consistently for someone you care about. For example, sending a daily message of encouragement or showing up on time.
- Reflect on how consistency builds trust over time in both relationships and personal goals.

6. Practice Nonverbal Communication

Horses rely heavily on body language and energy for communication. Develop your own nonverbal communication skills:

- Pay attention to your body language. Are you open and relaxed, or closed off and tense?
- Practice mirroring the energy of those around you. If someone is calm, match their calmness; if they're upset, offer grounding energy.
- Observe how people respond to your nonverbal cues.

7. Reflect on Your Herd

Mustangs thrive in herds, finding safety, support, and connection in their community. Reflect on your own "herd":

- Who are the people who offer you support and connection?
- Are there relationships that need nurturing or boundaries?
- Take a moment to express gratitude to those who form your community.

8. Embrace Your Authentic Self

Mustangs are unapologetically themselves. They remind us that authenticity is the key to genuine connection:

- Reflect on areas in your life where you might be hiding parts of yourself out of fear or insecurity.
- Practice showing up authentically in small ways, whether it's expressing an opinion, pursuing a passion, or setting a boundary.
- Celebrate your unique qualities and strengths, just as they are.

Closing Reminder

The lessons of the mustangs are as much about how we connect with ourselves as they are about how we connect with others. By observing, respecting boundaries, and showing up authentically, you create a foundation for trust and connection in every area of your life. Take these steps as a guide to living with greater presence, courage, and integrity.

CHAPTER 6

The Rubik's Cube of My Mind

The metaphor of the Rubik's cube came to me during one of those sleepless nights when my thoughts refused to settle. I hadn't sought it out, but there it was, vivid and insistent. The six-sided puzzle, each face representing a different aspect of my life—my past, my present, my relationships, my work, my fears, my hopes. Each twist and turn reflected the ways my mind was constantly rearranging itself, trying to find balance, trying to align.

I wasn't good at the actual Rubik's cube, the toy I'd struggled with as a child. It had always felt impossible, its endless permutations a source of frustration. But now, as I sat on my porch staring out at the horses, it felt like the perfect metaphor for what was happening within me.

The Puzzle of My Mind

My mind had been a puzzle for as long as I could remember. Thoughts looping, emotions spiraling, patterns repeating. I had spent years trying to make sense of it all, to "solve" myself. But every time I thought I was close, something shifted, and the colors scattered again. The frustration I had felt as a child trying to align the cube was the same frustration I felt now, trying to align the pieces of my inner world.

The horses, as always, offered a different perspective. They didn't overthink. They didn't analyze. They simply were. Their ability to live in the moment, to respond to what was in front of them without carrying the weight of the past or the anxiety of the future, was something I both admired and envied.

While the horses grounded me in the present, they also offered lessons in how to navigate the complexities of my own mind. Just as RC and Katniss found alignment through trust and patience, I realized my own journey mirrored theirs.

Finding Alignment

The process of "solving" the cube wasn't about perfection. It was about patience. I thought about the way I had worked with RC, my steadfast palomino, taking the time to rebuild our trust after the accident. It hadn't been a straight line. There had been setbacks, moments when I wondered if we were making any progress at all. But with each small step, we had moved closer to alignment.

I remembered a recent session with Katniss, a spirited mustang mare whose fear of being touched mirrored my own resistance to facing my fears. She had come to the ranch as a wild and traumatized 4-month-old filly, her body tense and her movements guarded. Over weeks of gentle work, she had begun to soften. One day, as I stood in the pasture, she approached me of her own accord, her head lowering in a gesture of trust. It was a breakthrough, a small but significant shift that reminded me of the power of presence and patience.

It was the same with my own journey. The twists and turns of my mind weren't something to fight against. They were part of the process, part of the realignment. Each twist revealed something new, a layer I hadn't seen before, an opportunity to grow.

One morning, after a particularly vivid dream about the Rubik's cube, I decided to sit with it, to let the metaphor unfold. I grabbed my journal and began to write; the words came in fits and starts:

"The cube has six faces. Each face is a part of me: the past, the present, my fears, my hopes, my relationships, my work. They're all connected, all intertwined. When one face moves, the others move, too. I can't isolate them, can't 'solve' one without affecting the others."

I paused, the pen hovering over the page. It was a simple truth, but one that felt profound in the moment. I had spent so much of my life compartmentalizing, trying to keep the different parts of myself separate. But that wasn't how life worked. Everything was connected. Every decision, every action, every thought rippled outward, affecting the whole.

The Nervous System's Dance

The Rubik's cube wasn't just a metaphor for my mind. It was a metaphor for the way my nervous system operated—the way it responded to stress, to fear, to change. I thought about the physical sensations I often experienced: the tightness in my chest, the racing of my heart, the heat that rose to my face when I felt overwhelmed. Those sensations weren't random; they were patterns my mind and body learned long ago, still protecting me even when the danger had passed.

My work with the horses gave me a framework for understanding it. When Asha, a once-wild mustang, went into "fight or flight" mode, it wasn't because she wanted to. It was because her nervous system had been triggered. The same was true for me. The moments when I felt panicked or stuck weren't signs of failure. They were signs that my system was trying to protect me, to keep me safe.

Just as I had worked with Asha to help her reset her nervous system through grounding and presence, I could do the same for myself.

Twists and Turns

I began to see the twists of the cube not as obstacles but as opportunities. Each twist revealed something new: a belief I needed to question, a pattern I needed to break, a wound I needed to heal. And with each twist, I felt myself moving closer to alignment.

One evening, as I sat with DreamCatcher in the pasture, I noticed the way the setting sun cast long shadows across the grass. Her breath fogged in the cool air as the fading sunlight reflected off her dark coat, a perfect blend of calm and strength. The colors of the sky—orange, pink, deep purple—reminded me of the cube, the way the hues shifted and blended.

It was beautiful, but it was also fleeting. The colors would change, the light would fade, and the moment would pass. But that was the nature of the cube, of life itself. It wasn't meant to be solved and set aside. It was meant to be lived, to be explored, to be appreciated for its complexity.

The voice of my Higher Self spoke softly, almost as if reading my thoughts:

"The cube doesn't need to be solved. It needs to be understood."

I smiled, the tension in my chest easing. I didn't have to have all the answers. I didn't have to get it "right." I only had to stay present, to stay curious, to keep turning the cube and learning from each twist.

Loving the Process

That night, I wrote in my journal:

"The Rubik's cube is my mind, my heart, my spirit. It's the way I move through the world, the way I respond to its challenges and joys. It's not a problem to be solved. It's a journey to be embraced. Each twist brings me closer to myself, closer to the truth of who I am. And I am learning, slowly but surely, to love every turn."

As I closed the journal, I felt a sense of peace I hadn't felt in years. The cube wasn't perfect, and neither was I. But both were works in progress, and that was more than enough.

Action Steps for Chapter 6: The Rubik's Cube of My Mind

This chapter explores the metaphor of the Rubik's cube as a reflection of the complexities of the mind and the journey toward alignment. The following action steps will help you engage with this metaphor, offering practical ways to better understand your inner workings and embrace the process of growth and self-discovery.

1. Create Your Own Rubik's Cube Metaphor

The Rubik's cube represents the interconnected aspects of your life. Begin by identifying the "faces" of your own personal cube.

How to Practice:

Take a piece of paper and draw a six-sided cube.

- How to Draw a Simple 3D Cube (Showing Three Sides):

  Start with the Front Face:
  Draw a square in the center of your paper. This will represent the front face of the cube.

  Draw the Back Face:
  Now, about an inch above and to the right (or left) of the first square, draw a second square of the same size. This will represent the back face of the cube.

Connect the Corners:

Next, draw four straight lines to connect the corresponding corners of the two squares:

- Connect the top left corner of the front square to the top left corner of the back square.
- Connect the top right corners.
- Connect the bottom left corners.
- Connect the bottom right corners.

Visualize the Three Visible Sides:

You should now see a simple 3D cube shape with three sides visible: the front, the top (or bottom), and one side. It will resemble a box or a die.

- Label each face with a major area of your life (e.g., past, present, relationships, fears, hopes, work), as explored in this chapter.
- Reflect on how these areas are interconnected. Write a sentence or two about how a change in one area impacts the others.

Why It Helps:

This exercise helps you visualize the interconnectedness of your life, fostering a deeper understanding of how each aspect influences the whole.

2. Pause and Observe Patterns

Your mind operates in patterns—some constructive, others limiting. Learn to observe these patterns without judgment.

How to Practice:

- The next time you feel overwhelmed or stuck, pause and ask yourself:
  - What pattern is playing out here?

- o   Is this pattern serving me, or is it holding me back?
- Write down your observations in a journal to identify recurring themes.

Why It Helps:

Recognizing patterns is the first step toward transforming them into opportunities for growth.

3. Engage in Nervous System Resets

Just as a horse's nervous system can be calmed through grounding techniques, you can reset your own nervous system when it becomes dysregulated.

How to Practice:

- Try a grounding exercise, such as the 5-4-3-2-1 technique:
  - o   Name 5 things you can see.
  - o   Name 4 things you can feel.
  - o   Name 3 things you can hear.
  - o   Name 2 things you can smell.
  - o   Name 1 thing you can taste.
- Pair this with slow, deep breathing to soothe your nervous system.

Why It Helps:

Resetting your nervous system creates space to approach challenges with clarity and calm.

4. Embrace the Twists

Every twist of the cube reveals something new. Learn to see these twists as opportunities rather than obstacles.

How to Practice:

- When faced with a challenge, pause and reflect:
  - What is this situation revealing about me?
  - What can I learn from this twist in my journey?

- Write down at least one lesson or insight gained from the experience.

Why It Helps:

Reframing challenges as opportunities fosters a mindset of growth and curiosity.

5. Practice Presence Through Horses

Horses embody presence and alignment. Use their wisdom to guide your journey toward inner alignment.

How to Practice:

- Spend time observing or interacting with a horse (or visualize the experience if you don't have access to one).
- Notice their calm presence, the way they move, and how they respond to their environment.
- Reflect on how you can bring that same sense of presence into your own life.

Why It Helps:

Connecting with the grounded energy of horses helps you cultivate a sense of calm and focus.

6. Journal to Understand Your Cube

Journaling is a powerful tool for self-discovery and reflection. Use it to explore the metaphor of your Rubik's cube.

How to Practice:

- Set aside 10 minutes to write about one "face" of your cube each day. Reflect on:
  - How does this area of my life affect others?
  - What patterns do I notice here?
  - What small step can I take to create alignment in this area?
- End each journaling session with a positive affirmation, such as, "I am a work in progress, and that is enough."

Why It Helps:
Journaling brings clarity and helps you connect with the deeper layers of your inner world.

7. Celebrate Progress, Not Perfection

The Rubik's cube teaches us that alignment is a process, not a destination. Celebrate small victories along the way.

How to Practice:

- At the end of each day, write down one thing you did well or one small step you took toward alignment.
- Reflect on how it made you feel and what it taught you about yourself.

Why It Helps:
Celebrating progress reinforces positive patterns and keeps you motivated on your journey.

Reflective Journal Prompts

1. What are the six "faces" of my Rubik's cube, and how do they interact with each other?

2. When I encounter a twist in my life, how can I approach it with curiosity and patience?
3. How can I honor my nervous system and create a sense of safety within myself?

Integrating Reminder

The Rubik's cube reflects the complexity of your inner world, showing how each twist holds the potential for growth and alignment. By engaging with these action steps, you'll learn to embrace the twists and turns of your mind with patience and understanding. Just as the cube isn't meant to be solved and set aside, your journey isn't about reaching perfection—it's about discovering the beauty in every step of the process.

CHAPTER 7

Walking Into the Unknown

The prison was gone, reduced to ashes and smoke. I stood there with the beautiful woman and the inner child, watching as the flames consumed it. My heart was a tangle of relief, grief, and anticipation. And then, hand in hand, we turned away, walking together into the great unknown.

It was a moment I had envisioned countless times, but now that it had arrived, the reality was unsettling. Freedom wasn't the absence of fear. It was choosing to move forward despite it.

The Edge of the Unknown

With the prison reduced to ashes, I was free, but freedom brought its own questions. Without the walls that once defined me, I was left standing at the edge of an open field, staring into the unknown. The world felt different—brighter, sharper, filled with possibilities I hadn't seen before. But with those possibilities came questions. Who am I without the prison? What does life look like now?

The beautiful woman and the inner child were with me, their presence a comfort. They didn't speak, but I felt their quiet encouragement. The woman radiated strength and grace, embodying everything I hoped to become. The child carried a sense of wonder, a reminder to stay curious and approach this new chapter with an open heart.

The unknown was both thrilling and terrifying. It was a blank canvas, a space where anything was possible. But it was also uncharted territory, a place where I would have to navigate without the familiar boundaries that had once kept me safe.

Lessons from the Herd

One morning, I sat by the fence, watching the herd as they moved through the pasture. The horses were a constant source of grounding, their presence a reminder of the lessons I had learned. They didn't worry about the unknown; they simply responded to the moment, trusting their instincts and their connection to one another.

Katniss caught my eye, her deep red sorrel coat shimmering in the sunlight, a testament to her strength and spirit. She had come to me as a terrified four-month-old filly, ripped from her mother during a brutal roundup that claimed the lives of all the mares. Unknown to us at the time, she had also suffered a broken neck in the chaos. She was wild and wary, carrying the weight of trauma no creature should endure.

Yet, over time, she allowed trust to take root. Step by step, she transformed from a frightened, untouchable soul into a powerful presence—a mustang who now helps women rise above their own pain, sorrow, and fear, reminding them to love life even in its hardest moments. Where Katniss taught me the courage to carry my past with grace, Troubadour reminded me of the quiet power of trust and presence.

Troubadour's Lesson: Rediscovering Trust

The turning point came with Troubadour, a stunning palomino rescued from a kill pen. Troubadour had been brought into my life at a time when I was still grappling with the reality of RC's neurological condition and the limitations it placed on our partnership. While my heart ached for what RC and I had lost, Troubadour's guarded demeanor forced me to be present in the moment.

When Troubadour arrived, he carried a deep mistrust, his past filled with abandonment and uncertainty. He was slow to approach, his amber eyes scanning me cautiously, as though he were weighing whether I could be trusted. I began, as always, with patience. I didn't force a connection. Instead, I let him come to me, giving him space to decide if I was worth his trust.

One morning, after weeks of quiet work in the pasture, Troubadour surprised me. As I sat in the grass with my journal, he approached from behind, his soft breath warm against my shoulder. He didn't nudge me or demand attention. He simply stood there, his presence a quiet acknowledgment of the trust we were building.

That moment wasn't dramatic, but it was profound. Troubadour had chosen to connect, not out of obligation but out of trust. In that small, quiet gesture, he reminded me that rebuilding faith—whether in others or in ourselves—is a process. It can't be rushed, but it's worth every moment of effort.

Embracing the Unknown

Troubadour's willingness to step into trust mirrored my own. I began to approach my life with the same mindset I used with the horses: patience, trust, and presence. I didn't need to have all the answers. I just needed to take the next step, and then the one after that.

The unknown wasn't a void to be feared; it was a space to be explored. It was where growth happened, where transformation took root. Each day brought new challenges, but it also brought new opportunities to learn, to connect, to create.

Writing the Future

One evening, I sat on the porch, my journal open on my lap. The sky was painted with the colors of sunset, the kind of beauty that always took my breath away. I began to write, the words flowing easily:

"The unknown is where life begins. It's where we find out who we are, not by knowing but by doing. By stepping forward, even when we're scared. By trusting that the path will reveal itself as we walk it."

I closed the journal and looked out at the horizon, a sense of peace settling over me. The prison was gone, the path ahead unwritten. But for the first time, I wasn't afraid of the unknown. I was ready to embrace it, one step at a time.

Action Steps for Chapter 7: Walking Into the Unknown

This chapter explores the profound transformation that comes from stepping into the unknown. The process is both thrilling and daunting, requiring courage, curiosity, and the willingness to embrace uncertainty. The following exercises will help you lean into this journey with intention and grace.

Action Step 1: Identify Your Unknowns

- Reflect on areas of your life where you feel called to step into the unknown:
  - Is it a career change? A new relationship? A personal challenge?

- Write down these areas in your journal, and beside each one, note what excites you and what scares you about taking that step.

Action Step 2: A Courage Inventory

- Make a list of moments in your life when you've faced the unknown and emerged stronger.
- Reflect on these questions:
  - What helped you move forward in those moments?
  - What strengths or resources did you draw upon?

- Use this inventory as a reminder of your capacity to face uncertainty.

Action Step 3: The Power of Curiosity

- Approach the unknown with a sense of curiosity rather than fear:
  - Choose one small unknown to explore this week (e.g., try a new activity, start a conversation with someone new, or approach a task differently).
  - Afterward, journal about the experience:
    What did you learn?
    How did it feel to step into something unfamiliar?

Action Step 4: Connect with a Trusted Guide

- Just as Katniss and Troubadour found strength and trust through connection, consider who or what in your life serves as a grounding force when facing uncertainty.
  - This might be a person, a pet, or even your own intuition.

- Reach out to this guide, whether it's seeking advice, spending time together, or simply acknowledging their presence as a source of support.

Action Step 5: A Visualization for Embracing the Unknown

- Find a quiet space and close your eyes.
- Imagine yourself standing at the edge of a vast, open field. Ahead lies the unknown—a place of endless possibilities.
- Picture yourself taking a step forward, feeling both the weight of fear and the buoyancy of faith.
- With each step, feel a growing sense of curiosity, excitement, and trust in the path ahead.
- End with the affirmation: "I am open to the unknown and trust the journey ahead."

Action Step 6: Anchor in the Present

- When fear or uncertainty feels overwhelming, practice grounding yourself in the present moment:
  - Take three deep breaths, focusing on the sensation of air moving in and out.
  - Name five things you can see, four things you can touch, three things you can hear, two things you can smell, and one thing you can taste.
  - Remind yourself that the unknown begins with one present moment at a time.

Integrating Chapter 7

Walking into the unknown is less about having all the answers and more about taking the next step with courage and curiosity. By practicing these action steps, you will begin to see the unknown not as something to fear but as an opportunity for growth and discovery.

CHAPTER 8

Reclaiming Your Power

The first thing I noticed about freedom was how weightless it felt. Without the walls of the prison, I could breathe more deeply, move more freely. But the absence of weight didn't mean the absence of challenge. Freedom brought with it a new responsibility—the responsibility to choose, to create, to step fully into my own power.

Power was not something I had always understood. For years, I had equated it with control: controlling outcomes, controlling relationships, controlling myself. But now, standing on the other side of the prison's ashes, I realized that real power wasn't about control. It was about alignment—about bringing my thoughts, actions, and beliefs into harmony with my Higher Self.

Trusting the Process

The journey of reclaiming my power began with small steps, much like my work with the horses. Trust had to be rebuilt—not trust in others, but trust in myself. I had spent so many years doubting my instincts, second-guessing my decisions, that the idea of trusting my inner voice felt foreign.

My time with Rocky had taught me the importance of listening. With horses, you couldn't force trust. You had to earn it, moment by moment, through patience and presence. I realized the same was true for my relationship with myself. Reclaiming my power wasn't about a dramatic transformation; it was about quiet consistency, about showing up for myself every day.

One morning, as I worked with Troubadour, the palomino who had come to me from a kill pen, I felt a shift. Troubadour had been guarded when he first arrived, his past filled with abandonment and rejection. I had given him time to process, to feel safe, to decide when he was ready to move forward. That day, as I guided him through a series of simple exercises, he responded with a confidence I hadn't seen before. His movements were fluid, his ears attentive. He was no longer reacting out of fear. He was responding with trust.

"That's it," I said softly, my voice filled with pride. "You've got this."

The realization hit me like a bolt of lightning: *So, do I.*

I had spent years reacting—reacting to fear, to shame, to the expectations of others. But now, I could feel myself shifting. I was no longer bound by those old patterns. I was learning to respond—with trust, with intention, with power.

Harry's Resilience: Choosing Joy Amid Challenge

The lessons I was learning mirrored Harry's story in so many ways. Handsome Harry, our Mustang Ambassador, had faced challenges that could have broken his spirit. As a foal, he was removed from the wild at just five days old, battling anemia and a lice infestation. He grew up bottle-fed, far from the open plains of his birthplace, and yet, from an early age, he radiated an unshakable zest for life.

Troubadour showed me the power of patience and trust, while Harry reminded me of the resilience needed to face life's challenges head-on. Together, their journeys mirrored the steps I was taking to reclaim my own power.

When Harry partially amputated his hoof in 2022, his future was uncertain. The injury was severe, and his recovery would be long and arduous. For weeks, his days were filled with pain management, bandage changes, and careful monitoring. The prognosis was guarded, but Harry approached each moment with a calm strength that inspired everyone around him.

There was a day, during one of his follow-up visits, when Harry rested his head against my chest, his soft breath warm against my skin. Despite everything he had endured, there was no trace of fear in his eyes—only trust and a quiet determination to keep moving forward. That moment reminded me of a truth I had often shared with others but now needed to embrace for myself: resilience isn't about erasing the pain. It's about choosing joy, even amid the challenges.

Harry's recovery wasn't just physical. It was emotional and spiritual—a journey of healing that redefined his role within our herd and deepened his bond with everyone who knew him. His willingness to rise above pain and embrace life's possibilities became a touchstone for my own journey of reclaiming power.

Redefining Power

The next challenge came in the form of my work. I had always been passionate about helping women and horses, but my fear of failure had often held me back. I worried about not being enough, about falling short of the expectations I had set for myself. But now, as I looked at my work through the lens of freedom, I began to see it differently.

My work wasn't about proving myself. It wasn't about achieving perfection. It was about connection—connecting with the women who came to me for guidance, connecting with the horses who mirrored their struggles and triumphs, and connecting with myself.

One evening, I sat down to revisit my program, Heart & Soul Connection. The name had evolved from its original title, Unbridled Freedom, to reflect the deeper purpose I now saw in my work. Heart & Soul Connection captured what I had come to see as the core of my work: aligning with the deeper truths within ourselves and fostering authentic connection with others.

I started by writing down the core principles that had guided my own transformation:

- Trust your instincts. Your inner voice is your greatest guide.
- Embrace the power of the pause. Growth happens in the space between.
- Stay present. Freedom exists in the here and now.
- Honor your journey. Every step, even the difficult ones, is part of your becoming.

As I wrote, I felt a sense of clarity and purpose. This was my power—not in controlling every outcome, but in sharing my story, my lessons, my heart.

A Circle of Connection

One of the most profound moments came during a session with a group of women who had come to my ranch for a retreat. They were gathered in a circle, sharing their stories of fear and resilience, of heartbreak and hope. The horses moved among them, their presence grounding and calming.

As one woman spoke about her struggle to find her voice, I felt a familiar ache in my chest. I had been there, silenced by doubt, afraid to speak my truth. I leaned forward, my voice steady but filled with emotion.

"You have more power than you realize," I said. "It's not about being fearless. It's about being willing. Willing to show up, willing to try, willing to fail. That's where your power lies—in the willingness to be who you are."

The woman's eyes filled with tears, and she nodded. It was a moment of connection, of shared understanding. And in that moment, I felt my own power growing, rooted not in control but in authenticity.

Power Through Presence

Reclaiming my power was an ongoing process. There were days when fear still whispered in my ear, when the old patterns tried to pull me back. But now, I had tools. I had the lessons of the horses, the guidance of my Higher Self, the support of the beautiful woman, and the inner child who walked beside me.

Power wasn't about being perfect. It was about being present. It was about choosing to show up, even when it was hard. It was about trusting that I had everything I needed within me.

One evening, as I sat by the pasture watching the horses graze, I felt a sense of peace I hadn't known before. Rocky's steady presence, Troubadour's resilience, Harry's joy, and the quiet strength of all the horses in my life reminded me of the power I was reclaiming.

I was free. I was powerful. And I was ready for whatever came next.

Action Steps for Chapter 8: Reclaiming Your Power

This chapter emphasizes the journey of reclaiming personal power—not through control or perfection but through alignment, trust, and consistent action. The following exercises are designed to help you reconnect with your inner strength and lead with authenticity.

Action Step 1: Define Your Power

- Reflect on what personal power means to you. Consider:
  - When do you feel most powerful?
  - What external factors influence your sense of power (positively or negatively)?

- Write a personal definition of power in your journal. Keep this as a touchstone for moments when you feel disconnected from your strength.
- Consider how Rocky, Troubadour, or Harry demonstrated their own forms of power—resilience, trust, and presence. Reflect on how these qualities resonate with your definition.

Action Step 2: A Daily Trust Practice

- Identify one small way to trust yourself each day:
  - This could be trusting your ability to make a decision, to say no, or to follow through on a promise to yourself.

- At the end of the day, journal about the experience:
  - What did trusting yourself feel like?
  - What was the outcome?

Action Step 3: Strength from the Past

- Recall a time when you faced a challenge and emerged stronger. Reflect on:
  - What internal resources did you draw upon?
  - How did you navigate the situation?

- Write about this experience, and identify how those same strengths can serve you in reclaiming your power today.

- As you reflect, think about Harry's journey and how he chose joy amid challenges. How have you done something similar in your own life?

Action Step 4: Grounding Through the Body

- Reclaiming power often begins with grounding yourself in the present moment. Practice a grounding exercise:
  - Stand barefoot on the ground, feeling the earth beneath you.
  - Close your eyes and take deep breaths, imagining your energy flowing downward like roots anchoring you to the earth.
  - Repeat the affirmation: "I am grounded, strong, and steady."
- Use this exercise whenever you feel disconnected or overwhelmed.

Action Step 5: Setting Boundaries

- Identify an area of your life where your boundaries feel unclear or overstepped:
  - This could be with a person, a situation, or even with yourself.
- Write down one boundary you want to set and why it matters to you.
- Take one small action to reinforce this boundary, such as having a conversation or changing a habit.

Action Step 6: The Power Pause

- Practice pausing before reacting in situations that trigger you:

o   When you feel frustration, anger, or doubt, pause and take three deep breaths.

o   Ask yourself: *What is the most empowering response I can choose right now?*

- Reflect on how the pause impacts your actions and sense of control.

Action Step 7: Visualize Your Power

- Find a quiet space and close your eyes.
- Picture a version of yourself standing tall, confident, and radiant with inner power.
- Visualize yourself handling challenges with ease, speaking your truth, and leading with clarity and grace.
- End with the affirmation: "My power comes from within. I trust myself to navigate life with strength and authenticity."

Integrating Chapter 8

Reclaiming your power is a practice that unfolds step by step. Through these action steps, you can build trust in yourself, anchor in your strengths, and align with the inner resources that have always been yours.

CHAPTER 9

The Gift of the Pause

The metaphor of the Rubik's cube still lingered in my mind, but its colorful complexity had been replaced by something simpler, quieter—a pause. It was Boomer, a towering wild buckskin mustang, who had taught me this lesson, though I hadn't realized it at first.

Boomer was a mustang with a history. His massive frame carried a lifetime of mistrust and solitude, scars visible to the eye and written in every guarded step he took. When he arrived at my ranch, the word was that he was "untrainable," a mustang who shut down under pressure or exploded into unpredictable reactions. To some, he was a challenge. To me, he was a mirror.

Boomer's journey began long before he came to my ranch. He had been removed from the Virginia Range at three years old, a lone stallion known for his extraordinary ability to jump fences and breed ranchers' mares. Twice relocated and twice returned to the wild, Boomer was finally removed permanently by the Department of Agriculture. I had brought him into my life because he was the grandson of a legendary wild mustang named Ghost, a stallion revered in Nevada for his majestic presence and determination to remain wild. Ghost's tragic death—struck by a motorcyclist on a summer evening—had only deepened my resolve to honor his legacy through Boomer. But I hadn't anticipated just how fiercely Boomer would embody his grandfather's spirit.

That particular day, the sky was overcast, the clouds hanging low like an unspoken tension. Boomer paced the edge of the round pen, his ears flicking nervously, his head held high, constantly threatening to go over the six-foot panels or through me. I had tried everything in my usual repertoire—softening my energy, adjusting my posture, giving him space—but nothing seemed to break through his barrier.

And then, I stopped.

It wasn't planned. It wasn't a strategy. It was instinct. I lowered my energy, took a deep breath, and stepped back. I didn't move. I didn't speak. I just stood there, present and still, letting the moment be what it was.

Boomer's pacing slowed. His steps became smaller, his movements less frantic. Finally, he stopped. His head lowered slightly, his ears flicking toward me as if asking a question. Then, for the first time, he turned to face me, his storm-colored eyes softening.

It wasn't dramatic. It wasn't a breakthrough moment in the cinematic sense. But it was everything. In that stillness, something shifted. The energy between us transformed. He had chosen me in that moment, not out of submission but out of curiosity and trust. And all it had taken was a pause.

That day marked the beginning of my relationship with pauses—not as voids but as powerful spaces of possibility. For so long, my life had been a race, a constant drive to prove myself, to achieve, to push through. Pausing felt counterintuitive, almost indulgent. But Boomer had shown me the truth: Pauses weren't the absence of action—they were the foundation for it.

Rhythm of Stillness

The horses had always known this. Their lives were a rhythm of motion and stillness, a balance of action and rest. They didn't rush. They didn't force. They moved when the moment called for it, and they paused when it didn't.

I began to see how this applied to my own life. The pauses became moments of recalibration, opportunities to listen—to my inner voice, to my body, to the world around me. They were where clarity was born, where transformation took root.

One day, as I worked with Gino, another of my horses, the lesson deepened. Gino had come into my life carrying years of abandonment and rejection. His movements spoke of a deep mistrust, as though he expected the world to fail him at every turn.

I had been working on getting him to walk calmly through an open gate—a seemingly simple task that felt monumental given his resistance. Gino would rush through, his body tense and his eyes wide. No amount of correction seemed to change his response.

And so, I paused.

I stepped back, letting go of my expectations and simply observing him. Gino stood by the gate, pawing the ground and snorting in frustration, but I didn't push. I waited. Slowly, he stopped pawing, his breathing steadied, and his muscles relaxed. When he finally looked at me, it was as though he was asking for permission to trust.

I raised my hand gently, inviting him forward without force. This time, Gino walked through the gate with a deliberate calm, pausing halfway to glance back at me as if to say, *I can do this.*

It wasn't just about the gate. It was about creating space for Gino to process his fear and find his footing. In Gino's pause by the gate, I saw the profound power of space—not just for him to process his fear, but for me to recognize the importance of letting go and allowing trust to grow naturally.

Finding the Gift

That evening, as I reflected on the day's events, the words poured out in my journal:

"The pauses are where the magic happens. They are where we find clarity, where we reconnect with ourselves and the world around us. They are not empty—they are full of potential. In the pauses, we find our strength, our balance, our truth."

Boomer's wildness wasn't a failure—it was his truth. His unyielding spirit reminded me that pauses don't always lead to predictable outcomes, but they always create space for authenticity and growth.

The pauses became a guiding principle, a cornerstone of my life and work. They showed up in the quiet moments before stepping into the round pen, in the stillness of early mornings by the pasture, in the space between breaths during meditation. They weren't just practices; they were acts of trust—trust in myself, in the process, in life.

Boomer's story didn't end with trust. Despite my best efforts, his wild spirit never fully settled into life with humans. Eventually, he was sent to a sanctuary where he could live out his days with others like him. He remained wild at heart, his fierce determination unbroken. But the time we spent together had left an indelible mark on my life. Boomer's legacy wasn't in his compliance but in his resistance, his unyielding spirit a reminder that some parts of us are meant to remain untamed.

The sun dipped below the horizon, casting the sky in shades of orange and pink. I closed my eyes and took a deep breath, letting the stillness of the moment fill me. The pauses, I realized, weren't just moments of rest. They were gifts—gifts that allowed me to be fully present, fully alive.

And in those pauses, I had found myself.

Action Steps for Chapter 9: The Gift of the Pause

This chapter emphasizes the importance of pausing—not as a moment of inaction but as a space to recalibrate, process, and move forward with clarity and intention. The following exercises will help you embrace the power of the pause in your daily life and interactions.

Action Step 1: Create a Pause Ritual

- Identify a natural pause point in your day (e.g., before a meal, when transitioning between tasks, or before responding in a conversation).
- Pause for 1–3 minutes during these moments:
  - Take a few deep breaths.
  - Ask yourself: *What am I feeling right now? What do I need?*
  - Notice the energy you're bringing into the moment. Can you lower your energy or adjust your posture, as Boomer taught, to create a sense of calm?

- Use these pauses to center yourself and move forward with intentionality.

Action Step 2: Journaling the Pause

- Reflect on moments when a pause has helped or could have helped you:
  - Was there a time you reacted impulsively and later regretted it?
  - Conversely, was there a moment you paused and felt the benefit?

- Write about these experiences in your journal. What did you learn about yourself in these moments?

Action Step 3: Practice Active Stillness

- Choose an activity that allows you to practice being still, such as sitting in nature, meditating, or observing your surroundings without judgment.
- During this time:
  - Focus on your breath or the sounds around you.
  - Resist the urge to check your phone or fill the stillness with action.
  - Reflect on how the horses move with a rhythm of motion and stillness. How can you integrate this balance into your own life?
- Reflect on how this active pause influences your thoughts and emotions.

Action Step 4: The Pause Before Reacting

- When faced with a triggering situation:
  - Take three deep breaths before responding.
  - Ask yourself: *What is the best way to approach this? What outcome do I want?*
- Notice how this pause changes the tone of your response and the dynamic of the situation.

Action Step 5: Reflect Through Nature

- Spend time observing an animal, a tree, or even the rhythm of the wind. Note how nature inherently integrates pauses and stillness:
  - For example, observe a bird pausing between flights or the stillness of a tree between gusts of wind.

- o As you observe nature, think of Boomer's wildness or Gino's pause by the gate. How do these moments mirror the natural rhythm of stillness and movement?

- Reflect on how these natural pauses contribute to balance and harmony in nature—and how they might apply to your life.

Action Step 6: Grounding the Nervous System

- If you feel overwhelmed, use the pause to calm your body:
  - o Place your feet flat on the ground and close your eyes.
  - o Take deep breaths, counting to four as you inhale, holding for four, and exhaling for four.
  - o Imagine your breath flowing through your body like a wave, washing away tension.

- Use this technique to reset during moments of stress or uncertainty.

Action Step 7: Pausing in Relationships

- Practice pausing in conversations:
  - o Before responding, take a breath and ensure your words align with your values and intentions.
  - o Use the pause to actively listen and understand the other person's perspective.

- Reflect on how pausing impacts your communication and connection with others.

Integrating Chapter 9

The power in the pause is transformative, creating space for clarity, connection, and growth. Through these action steps, you can integrate pauses into your life as moments of reflection and recalibration, enhancing your relationships and deepening your connection with yourself.

CHAPTER 10

Embracing Wholeness

The journey to freedom wasn't just about breaking free from the prison of my mind. It was about reclaiming and embracing all the parts of myself, even the ones I had tried to silence or discard. The radiant, beautiful woman; the tender, wary inner child; the fear, the joy, the doubt, the trust—they were all part of me. To truly embrace my freedom, I had to embrace them all.

This wasn't an easy realization. I had spent so much of my life trying to separate myself from the parts that felt too raw or imperfect, shoving them aside under layers of effort and achievement. But no matter how hard I tried to push them away, they lingered. Like shadows waiting for the light, they remained, patient and unmoving, until I finally turned to face them.

The horses, as always, had been my guides in this realization. They didn't compartmentalize themselves or judge their own fears or instincts. A horse wasn't less of itself because it hesitated or spooked. It didn't hide its vulnerability or strive for perfection. It simply was. Whole and complete in its authenticity.

If the horses could live that way, so could I.

The Lesson of Wholeness

It was Gino who became my mirror during this part of the journey. The copper red gelding had arrived at my ranch carrying a lifetime of rejection, his body tense with the memory of abandonment. He avoided touch, retreating into himself whenever anyone came near. His eyes, though wide and expressive, seemed to ask a heartbreaking question: *Am I enough?*

I recognized that question because I had asked it myself so many times. Gino's guarded movements mirrored my own struggles to trust, to let myself be seen.

Our work together began slowly, almost imperceptibly. I didn't ask for anything; I simply showed up. I spent hours sitting quietly by the fence, letting him see me, feel my presence. Gradually, he began to come closer—not out of obligation, but out of curiosity. Step by step, Gino started to let me in.

It wasn't a straight path. Some days he was playful, even bold, and other days, he pulled back, his fear overtaking his curiosity. I didn't rush him. I met him where he was, honoring his pace and his process. Slowly, as trust grew between us, I saw his walls begin to crumble. He started to move with more ease, his body and spirit softening in ways that took my breath away.

The turning point came one quiet morning in the pasture. I had gone out to check on the herd, the sunlight spilling over the hills like liquid gold. Gino stood apart from the others, his head low, his body relaxed. As I approached, he lifted his head and began to walk toward me.

I stopped, letting him decide what would happen next. Gino paused for a moment, then closed the distance between us. He rested his head against my chest, his breath warm and steady. It was a simple gesture, but it carried a profound message: *I see you. I trust you. I am enough.*

Tears welled in my eyes as I ran my hand along his neck. Gino had taught me something I hadn't fully understood before: wholeness wasn't about fixing what was broken. It was about embracing every piece of myself—the light and the shadow, the fear and the strength, the beauty and the mess.

As I stood there with Gino, I felt the presence of the beautiful woman and inner child. The woman stood tall beside me, a quiet strength radiating from her. The child, wide-eyed with curiosity, gently touched Gino's mane as though bonding with the same vulnerability we both shared. These presences weren't just symbolic; they influenced how I moved through my days. In moments of doubt, I felt the woman's steady strength anchoring me. In moments of fear, the child's wonder reminded me to stay open.

Sharing the Message

The lesson of wholeness wasn't just for me. It became the foundation of my work with the women who came to my ranch. During a retreat, one participant, a woman named Sarah, shared her story of struggling with self-worth. Sarah spoke of the pressure to be perfect, the fear of judgment, and the pain of feeling unworthy.

As Sarah spoke, I felt a deep resonance. I had walked that same path, carried that same weight. When it was my turn to share, I told Sarah about Gino and the lessons he had taught me.

"Wholeness isn't about erasing the parts of yourself that feel hard to love," I said. "It's about embracing them. It's about standing in the light and the shadow and saying, 'This is me.' The parts of you that feel messy or broken are the parts that make you human. And being human is beautiful."

As I spoke, I realized the depth of my own healing. By sharing my story with Sarah, I was affirming the truth I had worked so hard to embody.

Sarah's tears weren't just a response to the words—they were a reflection of the connection we had forged, a shared understanding of what it meant to be whole.

A New Way of Being

The journey to wholeness wasn't a destination. It was a practice, a way of being. It was in the pauses, the moments of trust, the steps into the unknown. It was in the way I showed up for myself, the way I honored my process, the way I embraced my freedom.

The beautiful woman and the inner child were no longer distant figures. They were part of me, walking beside me, their presence steady and strong. Together, we navigated this new chapter, creating a life rooted in authenticity and love.

As I sat on the porch that evening, watching the herd graze peacefully in the fading light, I thought of Gino, the horses, and my own reflection in their eyes. Each had taught me the strength of embracing vulnerability, the courage of choosing connection, and the beauty of being whole.

I was whole. I always have been. The journey hadn't made me whole; it had simply reminded me of the truth I had carried all along.

And in that truth, I found my freedom.

Action Steps for Chapter 10: Embracing Wholeness

This chapter emphasizes the journey toward embracing every part of ourselves—the light and shadow, the fear and strength, the beauty and vulnerability. The following exercises will help you begin integrating and accepting all aspects of who you are.

Action Step 1: Identifying Your Parts

- Reflect on the different "parts" of yourself—the roles, identities, or aspects of your personality that you've embraced or hidden. For example:
    o The confident leader
    o The shy child
    o The perfectionist
    o The dreamer

- Write down each part and how it contributes to your life, positively or negatively.
- Ask: *What does each part need from me? How can I honor or integrate it?*
- Inspired by Gino's trust-building process, approach your parts with patience, letting them come forward in their own time.

Action Step 2: Wholeness Visualization

- Sit in a quiet space where you won't be interrupted.
- Close your eyes and imagine yourself standing in a circle of light, surrounded by all the parts of you.
    o Visualize them stepping into the circle one by one, bringing their unique gifts and challenges.
    o Picture the confident woman, the curious child, and any other parts of yourself joining the circle.

- Imagine welcoming them all, saying: "You are part of me, and I honor you."
- Reflect on how it feels to acknowledge every aspect of yourself and the strength it brings.

Action Step 3: Dialogue with the Inner Critic

- Identify a recurring critical voice or thought in your mind (e.g., *I'm not good enough* or *I'll never get this right*).
- Write down a dialogue between you and this inner critic:
  o Ask it why it's there and what it's trying to protect you from.
  o Respond with compassion, thanking it for its intentions but setting boundaries.

- Reflect on how engaging with this voice might soften its impact, much like how Gino softened when met with patience and trust.

Action Step 4: Embracing the Shadow

- Identify a quality or behavior you've judged or suppressed in yourself (e.g., anger, jealousy, or fear).
- Reflect on:
  o What triggers this quality?
  o How does it serve or protect you?
  o How might you express it in a healthy way?

- Write about how accepting this shadow could help you feel more whole, drawing on the narrator's realization that wholeness is about honoring every piece of yourself.

Action Step 5: Gratitude for Your Journey

- List three experiences, challenges, or parts of yourself that you've struggled to accept.
- For each, write a statement of gratitude, focusing on what you've learned or how it has shaped you. For example:
  o "I'm grateful for my perfectionism because it shows me how much I care about doing my best."

o "I'm grateful for my fear because it has taught me how to be brave."

- Reflect on how gratitude shifts your perspective and allows you to embrace your wholeness.

Action Step 6: Honoring Your Body

- Spend a few moments each day connecting with your body:
  o Place your hand over your heart or on your stomach and take deep breaths.
  o Thank your body for carrying you through life, despite its imperfections.

- Reflect on how your physical body is part of your wholeness— how it connects to your emotions, memories, and experiences, as Gino's body language reflected his emotions.

Action Step 7: Connect Through Creativity

- Choose a creative activity that allows you to express your wholeness—painting, writing, dancing, or even building something with your hands.
- As you create, focus on embracing all parts of yourself, letting the process (not the result) guide you.
- Reflect on what this creative act revealed about your inner world and how it connects to the stories of the horses and Sarah's journey toward self-acceptance.

Integrating Chapter 10

Embracing wholeness is a journey of acceptance and integration, not perfection. By honoring each part of yourself, you'll discover the strength and beauty in your authenticity, creating space for a deeper connection with yourself and others.

CHAPTER 11

The Voice of the Higher Self

The voice of my Higher Self had always been there, whispering in moments of stillness, nudging me toward growth, offering clarity when the noise of life became too loud. But for much of my life, I had ignored it. I had drowned it out with doubt, with fear, with the relentless drive to prove myself. It wasn't until I burned down the prison of my mind that I realized just how much I had silenced my own inner wisdom.

Now, standing in the freedom of my new life, I was learning to listen.

The journey began with small, almost imperceptible moments. Sometimes the voice was a quiet nudge, a sense that I should take a different path or approach a situation differently. Other times, it was a feeling deep within my chest, a knowing that came without logic but with unmistakable clarity. My Higher Self wasn't just instinct or intuition; it was felt deep within my heart—a still, quiet calmness filled with inner peace, certainty, and excitement all at the same time. It wasn't loud or demanding. It didn't argue. It simply waited, patient and unwavering.

But the challenge wasn't in hearing the voice—it was in trusting it.

I thought back to the times I had ignored my Higher Self. There had been moments when it had tried to guide me—a persistent discomfort in a toxic relationship, an intuitive pull to leave a job long before I did, the quiet knowing that I needed to rest even as I pushed myself harder. Each time I ignored it, the lessons that followed had been more painful, more difficult, until I could no longer deny the truth.

Working with horses had given me a practice ground for listening—not just with my ears, but with my whole being. Horses spoke through the flick of an ear, the shift of a hoof, the depth of their breathing. They mirrored emotions and reflected the truth with an honesty that left no room for pretension. I realized that the voice of my Higher Self spoke the same language: subtle, intuitive, rooted in presence.

If I could learn to listen to the horses, I could learn to listen to myself.

The first real test came during a retreat. A group of women had gathered at my ranch, each carrying their own struggles, their own fears, their own longing for connection. As their guide, I felt the weight of responsibility to give them answers, to ensure they left transformed. But as I watched them interact with the horses, the voice of my Higher Self whispered a different truth: "You don't need to have all the answers. You only need to hold space."

The words were a revelation. Just as I had learned with the horses, transformation wasn't about control or direction—it was about creating an environment where trust could grow. The same was true for the women. My role wasn't to fix or heal them; it was to create a space where they could find their own answers.

One woman, Laura, stood out. Quiet and reserved, she lingered on the edges of the group, her presence heavy with an unspoken burden. On the second day of the retreat, I found Laura standing by the fence, watching Dakota graze. The mustang mare had been a symbol of strength and resilience to so many, her presence grounding and steady. Laura seemed drawn to her, though she kept her distance.

I approached Laura slowly, sensing the vulnerability in her stillness. "You don't have to say anything," I said softly. "Just be here. Let yourself feel."

For a long time, Laura didn't respond. But then, tears began to well in her eyes. "I've spent my whole life feeling like I don't belong," she said finally. "Like there's no place for me."

The words hit me like an echo of my own past. I knew that pain, that doubt, that yearning for belonging. But I also knew the strength it took to speak those words aloud.

I didn't try to fix it. I didn't offer advice or platitudes. I simply placed a hand over my heart and said, "You belong. You always have. The world wouldn't be the same without you."

That evening, as I reflected on the day, the voice of my Higher Self returned. "This is your gift—not fixing, but witnessing. Not guiding, but holding space. Trust the process."

It was a message I needed as much for myself as for the women I worked with. For so much of my life, I had felt the need to control, to direct, to have the answers. But true connection didn't come from control—it came from trust.

My connection to my Higher Self deepened as I continued to practice listening. Each morning, I began with a moment of stillness, placing a hand over my heart and asking, *What do I need to know today?* Sometimes, the answers came as words. Other times, they came as a feeling, a memory, or an image. And always, they came with a quiet certainty that felt like home.

One morning, as I worked with RC, the palomino who had been my teacher through so many seasons of my life, I felt the voice guide me again. RC had been hesitant that day, his movements uncertain. Instead of pushing him forward, I stopped. I stood still, letting the moment unfold. Slowly, RC stepped closer, his head lowering in quiet trust.

"This is the way," the voice said. "Patience. Presence. Trust."

That evening, I wrote in my journal:

"The voice of the Higher Self is the voice of truth. It's not something outside of us—it's who we are. It whispers in the quiet moments, waiting for us to listen. And when we do, it leads us back to ourselves, to our wholeness, to our freedom."

The journey of listening to my Higher Self wasn't over. It was a practice; one I carried with me every day. Each step I took, each choice I made, was an act of trust—not in some external force, but in myself.

The voice was always there, steady and unwavering, guiding me toward the life I was meant to live. And now, with the prison behind me and the path ahead wide open, I was ready to listen.

My Higher Self would guide me.

It always had.

Action Steps for Chapter 11: The Voice of the Higher Self

This chapter invites you to tune into the voice of your Higher Self—the inner wisdom that guides you toward alignment, truth, and authenticity. The following exercises will help you strengthen your connection with this quiet, calm presence.

Action Step 1: Morning Connection Ritual

- Begin each morning with a moment of stillness.
    - Place your hand over your heart and take three deep breaths.
    - Ask yourself: *What does my Higher Self want me to know today?*

- Listen for the response—it might come as a word, a feeling, or an image.
- Write down whatever comes to you, no matter how small or abstract.

Action Step 2: Differentiating Voices

- Identify different "voices" in your mind—the inner critic, the doubter, the worrier, and the Higher Self.
- When faced with a decision or challenge, write out what each voice says.
  - Ask: Which voice feels calm, certain, and expansive?
- Practice choosing the voice of your Higher Self over the others.

Action Step 3: Journaling with Your Higher Self

- Start a dialogue with your Higher Self in your journal:
  - Write a question, such as: "What guidance do you have for me?" or "What should I focus on today?"
  - Allow the response to flow naturally, as if your Higher Self is writing back to you.
- Reflect on the insights or clarity that emerge from this practice.

Action Step 4: Trusting Your Intuition

- Recall a recent moment when you had an intuitive nudge but didn't follow it. Write about what stopped you and what the outcome was.
- Reflect on times when you did trust your intuition—what happened? How did it feel?
- Commit to trusting your intuition in one small way this week, such as choosing a new route, saying yes or no to something based on instinct, or taking a risk that feels right.

Action Step 5: Meditation to Hear Your Higher Self

- Find a quiet space and sit comfortably. Close your eyes and take slow, deep breaths.
- Visualize a light in your heart, growing brighter with each breath.
- Silently ask, *What do I need to know right now?* Allow your mind to quiet and let the answer arise naturally.
- Afterward, write down any thoughts, feelings, or images that came to you during the meditation.

Action Step 6: Embodying Your Higher Self

- Throughout your day, pause and ask: *What would my Higher Self do in this moment?*
    - How would your Higher Self respond to stress, make decisions, or treat others?

- Practice embodying this response, even if it feels small or imperfect.
- Reflect on how these moments of alignment shift your energy and perspective.

Action Step 7: Affirmations for Alignment

- Create affirmations that resonate with the voice of your Higher Self. For example:
    - "I trust myself to make the right choices."
    - "I am guided by wisdom and love."
    - "I listen to the quiet voice within me."

- Repeat these affirmations daily, especially when doubt or fear arises.

Integrating Chapter 11

The voice of the Higher Self is always present, patiently waiting for you to listen. By practicing stillness, trusting your intuition, and embodying its wisdom, you can align more deeply with your true self. Through this connection, you'll navigate life with greater clarity, authenticity, and peace.

CHAPTER 12

The Dance of Faith and Fear

Freedom didn't mean the absence of fear. It meant learning to coexist with it, to see it not as an enemy but as a teacher. Fear challenged me, pushed me, and forced me to grow. But alongside fear, there was faith— a steady, unyielding presence that reminded me of the bigger picture.

Faith and fear weren't adversaries. They were partners in an intricate dance, and my journey was about learning to move gracefully between them.

Fear often arrived unannounced, in whispers during moments of stillness or as a roar in the times I felt most vulnerable. It questioned my choices, my worth, and my ability to succeed. *What if you're not enough?* it would ask. *What if you fail?*

But I no longer ran from those questions. I had learned to pause, to listen to my Higher Self, to trust the process. And in those moments of stillness, faith would rise to meet me, whispering a quiet but certain response: "You are enough. Trust yourself."

One unforgettable lesson came during a session with Dakota, the mustang mare who had become the matriarch of my herd and a profound teacher. Dakota was a mare of contrasts—strong and steadfast, yet deeply intuitive and sensitive. One windy afternoon, we worked in the round pen, the gusts stirring both our energy and Dakota's instinct to bolt.

Her movements were sharp and unpredictable, her body taut with the tension of perceived danger. Fear crept into my chest as I watched

Dakota pace, her hooves striking the ground in rhythm with my own rising doubts. *What if I can't handle this? What if I fail her?*

I closed my eyes and took a deep breath, grounding myself in the moment. The voice of fear was familiar, but so was the voice of faith. "You've got this," it whispered. "Trust her. Trust yourself."

Instead of pushing Dakota or trying to contain her energy, I chose to meet her where she was. I softened my posture, relaxed my energy, and let Dakota move. Slowly, her pacing slowed. Her head lowered, her eyes softened, and she turned to face me, the tension melting into trust.

It was a moment of grace—a reminder that fear didn't need to be silenced or defeated. It needed to be understood, danced with.

As the days turned into weeks, I began to see fear differently. It wasn't a sign of weakness or failure; it was a sign of stepping into something new. Fear was the edge of growth, the signal that I was on the brink of transformation.

Faith, on the other hand, was the bridge that carried me across that edge. It reminded me that I didn't need to have all the answers, that the path would reveal itself as I walked it.

One morning, as I sat by the pasture, watching the herd graze, I reflected on the moments in my life when fear had been at its loudest. There was the time I had taken on my first wild mustang, unsure if I had the skill to connect with such a raw and untamed spirit. The time I launched my first retreat, terrified that no one would show up. The time I stood at the edge of my own mental prison, striking the match that would burn it down.

In each of those moments, fear had been present. But so had faith. And every time, faith carried me through.

The horses lived this dance every day. As prey animals, fear was woven into their DNA, an instinctive response to potential danger. But they also trusted—trusted their herd, their instincts, the humans who earned their respect. Watching them, I saw how seamlessly they moved between fear and faith, how they used fear as a tool to stay alert but didn't let it consume them.

I realized I could do the same.

I thought of Harry, who had faced incredible odds after his accident. The fear of his injury, the uncertainty of recovery, and the vigilance required to care for him had all loomed large. But alongside those fears was an undeniable faith—in his resilience, in the bond we shared, in the belief that he could heal. Harry had embraced his new normal with a joy and trust that inspired everyone who met him. He hadn't fought against the challenges; he had danced with them, showing me the strength that comes from accepting what is and stepping forward anyway.

That evening, I wrote in my journal: "Fear is a teacher. Faith is a guide. Together, they lead us to growth. Fear reminds us of what matters, of what's at stake. Faith reminds us that we are capable, that we are enough. The dance between them is not a battle—it's a partnership. And when we learn to move with both, we find our strength."

The next day, I shared this insight with a group of women during a retreat. We were gathered in a circle; their faces etched with the weight of their own fears. I spoke about my session with Dakota, about the moments when fear had felt insurmountable, and how faith had guided me through.

"You don't have to choose between faith and fear," I said. "You can hold both. Fear will challenge you, but faith will carry you. And together, they'll lead you to places you never thought you could go."

One of the women, Hannah, raised her hand. "But how do you keep faith when fear feels so overwhelming?"

I smiled, placing a hand over my heart. "You listen to the voice of your Higher Self. You pause. You breathe. And you remind yourself that fear is temporary. Faith is what lasts."

Hannah nodded, her eyes glistening with unshed tears. It was a moment of connection, a moment of shared humanity.

The dance of faith and fear wasn't something I had mastered—it was something I practiced every day. It showed up in my work with the horses, in my relationships, in my own journey of healing and growth. But now, I no longer saw fear as the enemy. I saw it as a partner, a necessary step in the dance.

As I sat on the porch that evening, the sky painted with the colors of sunset, I felt a deep sense of peace. The path ahead was still uncertain, still filled with challenges. But I knew I had everything I needed to navigate it. I had faith, I had fear, and I had the wisdom to move with both.

And in that dance, I found my freedom.

Action Steps for Chapter 12: The Dance of Faith and Fear

This chapter explores the interplay between faith and fear—the dance that defines growth and transformation. These exercises will help you recognize, understand, and balance these forces in your life.

Action Step 1: Naming Your Fears

- Make a list of the fears that hold you back—both big and small.
  - Include fears related to personal growth, relationships, career, or other areas of life.

- For each fear, write down:
  - Is this fear rational, primal, or irrational?
  - What is this fear trying to protect you from?

- Reframe each fear as an opportunity for growth. Example: "This fear is challenging me to step into my potential."

Action Step 2: Writing a Letter to Your Fear

- Choose one fear from your list and write a letter to it.
  - Address the fear directly: "Dear Fear, I see you."
  - Thank it for its role in keeping you safe.
  - Gently explain why it's no longer needed in this situation.

- After writing, reflect on whether this process shifts your perspective on fear.

Action Step 3: Cultivating Faith

- Reflect on moments in your life when you choose faith over fear.
  - What happened? How did it feel?

- Write down three affirmations that reinforce your faith, such as:
  - "I trust the path ahead, even if I can't see it clearly."
  - "I am strong enough to face uncertainty."
  - "Faith is my bridge to growth."

- Repeat these affirmations whenever fear arises.

Action Step 4: Visualizing the Dance

- Close your eyes and visualize faith and fear as partners in a dance.
  - Imagine fear stepping forward and faith guiding it back into balance.

- See yourself gracefully navigating the dance, moving fluidly between the two.

- After the visualization, write down any insights or feelings that arose.

Action Step 5: Fear as a Teacher

- Identify a recent situation where fear felt overwhelming.
  - Ask yourself: What did this fear teach me?

- Write down one lesson you've learned from this fear and how you can use it as a guide moving forward.
- Commit to seeing fear as a teacher rather than an obstacle.

Action Step 6: Stepping Forward in Faith

- Choose one small action that feels aligned with faith but stretches you out of your comfort zone.
  - It could be having a difficult conversation, trying something new, or making a decision you've been putting off.

- Take the action and reflect afterward:
- How did fear show up during this process?
- How did faith support you?

Action Step 7: Creating a Fear and Faith Journal

- Dedicate a journal to tracking your experiences with fear and faith.
  - Write about moments when fear tried to hold you back and how you responded.
  - Document instances when faith carried you forward.

- Over time, look for patterns in how you navigate this dance. Celebrate your progress.

Integrating Chapter 12

Fear and faith are not enemies but partners in growth. By learning to honor both and trusting the process, you can navigate life's uncertainties with grace and courage.

CHAPTER 13

Breaking the Cycle

Breaking free from old patterns is never a clean, linear process. It's messy, raw, and often feels like stumbling forward in the dark. For me, the cycles of self-sabotage had become so deeply woven into my identity that unraveling one thread often disrupted others I hadn't anticipated. But each unraveling, no matter how uncomfortable, revealed something essential—a deeper truth about myself and my journey.

The origins of those patterns lay in my childhood, though at the time, I couldn't have recognized them for what they were. Survival had meant being quiet, compliant, and invisible. It meant anticipating the needs of others while suppressing my own. Those early adaptations helped me navigate the chaos of my upbringing, but as I grew older, they became chains that bound me.

My need to prove myself, to seek external validation, and to push myself beyond my limits all stemmed from deeply ingrained beliefs about my worth. For years, the cycle repeated: inspiration would ignite my heart, and I'd dive in headfirst, my relentless drive fueling my actions. But as the pressure mounted, so did my self-doubt. *Am I good enough? Will this work? What if I fail?* The questions, persistent and insidious, would grow louder until fear paralyzed me. Exhaustion followed, and I would retreat, questioning everything. Time and again, the cycle ended in defeat. Yet each time I stepped away, I felt the quiet pull of hope urging me to try again.

The Three Types of Fear

In Chapter 12, I explored fear as a complex teacher, capable of revealing what matters most when approached with curiosity and compassion. But understanding fear more deeply became my pathway to freedom. I realized it wasn't a singular force; it was multifaceted, manifesting in different ways depending on the situation. This understanding was key to breaking free from the cycles that held me captive. I began to see fear not as the enemy, but as a spectrum of experiences, each with its own role and purpose.

There was Rational Fear, the kind that warned me of real and imminent threats. It was the fear that made me cautious when handling unpredictable situations with the horses or that heightened my senses when walking alone in the dark. Rational Fear was a protector, a necessary ally.

Then there was Primal Fear, the innate and instinctual fear hardwired into my brain. Primal Fear was rooted in survival, shaped by my earliest experiences of chaos and harm. It was the fear ignited in my childhood, reinforced by the trauma of being molested by the babysitter's son and the emotional, mental, and physical abuse that followed. This fear ran deep, often surfacing in moments when I felt vulnerable or exposed, whispering the age-old lie that children were to be seen and not heard.

Finally, there was Irrational Fear, the kind that defied logic but felt just as real. This was the fear that fed my self-doubt, questioning my every move and ability. It whispered, *You'll never be enough*, even when evidence pointed to the contrary. Irrational Fear often disguised itself as truth, but it was nothing more than a shadow of old stories I had outgrown.

Understanding these distinctions was a revelation. Each type of fear had a different voice, a different role, and not all deserved the same weight. Rational Fear deserved acknowledgment and respect; it kept me safe. Primal Fear needed compassion and healing, a recognition of its origins, and a chance to be soothed. Irrational Fear needed boundaries, a firm but gentle reminder that it no longer had control over my choices.

Fear was no longer a singular entity—it was a spectrum. This clarity allowed me to identify the fears that kept me trapped in old patterns. I could see how primal fears had been shaped by childhood trauma, how irrational fears had fueled my self-doubt, and how rational fears often got tangled in their shadow. Naming them, acknowledging their presence, became the first step in untangling their hold.

One morning, while preparing for a presentation at work, I felt the familiar wave of fear tighten my chest. My inner voice whispered, *What if I mess up? What if they don't respect me?* This time, instead of spiraling, I paused. I named the fear: "You're irrational. You're not rooted in truth." Then I asked myself: *What if this fear is simply a remnant of the stories I was told as a child?* With that acknowledgment, the tension eased. I went on to give the presentation with confidence I hadn't felt in years.

Daisy: A Mirror of Patterns

My work with the horses provided a living metaphor for breaking the cycle. Daisy, a skittish and reactive mare, became my mirror. Daisy had a habit of bolting whenever she felt overwhelmed, her movements unpredictable and erratic. Labeled as "difficult" by her previous handlers, Daisy had been dismissed as a problem to solve or avoid.

But I didn't see Daisy as a problem. I saw her as a teacher.

Our sessions were slow and filled with moments of uncertainty, but each pause, each hesitation, held a lesson. Daisy taught me the value of patience, of meeting her where she was rather than where I wanted her to be.

When Daisy bolted, I didn't react with frustration or force. I waited. I let her process, find her footing, and return when she was ready. In those pauses, trust began to grow.

Watching Daisy, I saw my own patterns reflected back at me. The bolting, the fear, the hesitation—it was all part of the same cycle. And just as I gave Daisy the space to pause and reset, I began to offer myself the same grace.

Breaking the Cycle

One afternoon, after a particularly challenging session with Daisy, I sat in the pasture, watching the horses graze. The sun was warm on my skin, the air alive with the hum of insects and the rustle of grass. Daisy moved among the herd with an ease that belied the tension she had shown earlier.

As I watched, a wave of clarity washed over me. Breaking the cycle wasn't about fighting it. It wasn't about forcing myself to be different or pretending the patterns didn't exist. It was about recognizing them, understanding them, and choosing a new path.

It was about meeting myself with the same patience and compassion I offered to Daisy.

The journey wasn't without setbacks. There were days when the old patterns reasserted themselves, when perfectionism or self-doubt clawed their way back into my thoughts. But now, I had the tools to navigate those moments. I paused, breathed, and reminded myself that growth wasn't about getting it right every time. It was about showing up, again and again.

Action Steps for Chapter 13: Breaking the Cycle

That evening, I wrote in my journal:

"Breaking the chains within isn't about perfection. It's about persistence. It's about choosing, moment by moment, to step out of the old patterns and into something new. It's about meeting yourself with patience and compassion, trusting that the process will unfold in its own time. And it's about remembering that you are worthy of the freedom you seek."

In Chapter 12, I delved into the role of fear in our lives—not as an enemy to be conquered, but as a teacher and guide. Fear often holds the keys to understanding what matters most to us, but only if we learn to listen and respond with curiosity and compassion. These action steps are designed to help you identify, explore, and work with your fears in a way that fosters growth and resilience.

1. Identify and Categorize Your Fears

Not all fears are the same. Begin by identifying and categorizing the fears in your life:

- **Rational Fear:** What fears are based on real, immediate dangers? For example, fear of falling when walking on ice.
- **Primal Fear:** What fears feel deeply ingrained or instinctual, such as fear of heights or dark places?
- **Irrational Fear:** What fears arise without a logical basis or seem tied to specific situations or triggers, such as fear of public speaking or rejection?

Write each fear under its category and reflect on how it impacts your thoughts, actions, and decisions.

2. Name and Acknowledge Your Fear

Fear often feels overwhelming when left unnamed. Practice identifying and naming your fear to gain clarity and create distance from it:

- What is the fear trying to protect me from?
- What story is my fear telling me?

For example, if you're afraid of failure, your fear might be saying, *If I fail, I'll lose respect or love.* Writing this down can help you see the fear objectively.

3. Explore the Wisdom of Fear

Fear often highlights areas where growth or attention is needed. Use the following questions to explore its wisdom:

- What is this fear trying to teach me?
- Is there a real threat, or is this fear based on a belief or assumption?
- What would I do if I weren't afraid?

This process transforms fear into an opportunity for self-awareness and growth.

4. Create a Safe Space for Fear

Fear is easier to work with when you feel grounded and supported. Create a physical or emotional space where you can explore your fears safely:

- Sit in a quiet, comfortable place and take a few deep breaths.

- Imagine fear as a presence sitting beside you. Visualize yourself asking it questions calmly, like you would a friend.
- Practice saying, "Thank you for trying to protect me. I see you, but I don't need you to control this situation."

This practice helps you develop a relationship with fear instead of letting it dominate you.

5. Take Small, Courageous Steps

Facing fear doesn't mean eliminating it entirely. It means taking small, manageable steps forward despite its presence:

- Identify one small action that challenges your fear but feels achievable. For example, if you fear public speaking, start by sharing your thoughts in a small group.
- Celebrate your courage after taking each step, no matter how small. Acknowledge your progress with kindness and pride.

Consistency in small actions builds resilience and reduces fear's hold over time.

6. Practice Fear-Soothing Techniques

When fear feels overwhelming, use these techniques to calm your mind and body:

- **Grounding:** Focus on your senses by naming five things you can see, four you can touch, three you can hear, two you can smell, and one you can taste.
- **Breathing:** Take slow, deep breaths, inhaling for a count of four, holding for four, and exhaling for six.
- **Movement:** Engage in a calming activity like yoga, walking, or stretching to release tension.

Regular practice of these techniques helps you respond to fear with clarity and calmness.

7. Journal Your Journey with Fear

Keep a journal dedicated to your experiences with fear. Reflect on:

- Moments when fear arose and how you responded.
- Insights you've gained about yourself through exploring fear.
- Actions you've taken despite fear and how they made you feel.

Journaling creates a record of your growth and reminds you of your strength in navigating challenges.

Closing Reminder

Fear is not a flaw or weakness; it's a natural part of being human. By listening to fear and responding with intention, you transform it from a source of limitation into a catalyst for growth. These steps are here to help you face your fears with compassion and courage, opening the door to a life of greater freedom and authenticity.

CHAPTER 14

The Role of Community

Community had always been a paradox for me—something I craved yet often resisted. Growing up, relationships were shaped by survival, by anticipating others' needs while suppressing my own. This left me longing for connection but hesitant to truly lean on anyone. Freedom, I thought, was something I had to achieve on my own.

It wasn't until my work with the horses—and the women who came to the ranch—that I realized how essential community was for healing and transformation. The horses thrived in their herds, finding safety and connection in one another. Watching them, I began to see that humans, at their core, weren't so different. We, too, needed our herd to thrive.

The Retreat: A Circle of Connection

The lesson first became clear during one of my retreats. A group of eight women had gathered at the ranch, each carrying their own burdens. Some had come to reconnect with themselves after years of prioritizing others. Others sought healing from past traumas. All of them, in their own way, were searching for freedom.

The retreat's itinerary was carefully planned: exercises designed to help the women connect with the horses and, in turn, with themselves. What I hadn't anticipated was how deeply the women would connect with one another.

On the second day, we gathered in a circle under the shade of an ancient oak tree. The horses grazed nearby, their presence grounding and calming.

I invited each woman to share her story, to speak her truth in a space of trust and non-judgment.

One by one, the women opened up. There were tears, laughter, and moments of silence as we absorbed the weight of each other's words. What struck me most was the way they supported one another—not with solutions or advice, but with presence. A hand on a shoulder. A nod of understanding. A whispered "Me too."

By the end of the day, something had shifted. The women who had arrived as strangers were now a community, bound by shared vulnerability and strength. It was a reminder that healing wasn't something to be done in isolation. Healing happened in connection, in relationship, in spaces where we allowed ourselves to be truly seen.

Lessons from the Herd

My work with the horses mirrored this truth. In the wild, horses relied on their herds for survival. They moved as one, each member playing a role in the group's safety and well-being. Even in captivity, the herd dynamic remained essential. Horses, deeply relational beings, found their sense of security in connection with one another.

I saw this dynamic play out in my own herd. RC, my wise and steadfast gelding, acted as the grounding force. Harry, playful and confident, brought a sense of lightness and curiosity. And DreamCatcher, the sage-like matriarch, carried an unyielding strength that inspired all who met her. Each horse brought something unique to the herd, and their relationships were a delicate balance of strength and vulnerability.

Watching them, I began to understand the role of community in my own life. I didn't have to do everything alone. I didn't have to carry the weight of my journey in isolation. Just as the horses leaned on one another, I could lean on the people who loved and supported me.

Moments of Transformation

The lesson wasn't just for me—it was for the women who came to the ranch. Over time, I began to weave the theme of community into my retreats and programs. I encouraged the women to support one another, to share their stories, to see their struggles and triumphs reflected in each other.

One powerful moment came during a retreat when a woman named Emily spoke about her fear of being vulnerable. Emily had always been the strong one, the caretaker, the one who held everything together. Letting others see her pain felt like a betrayal of that role.

As Emily spoke, another woman, Sarah, reached out and took her hand. "You don't have to be strong all the time," Sarah said gently. "We've got you."

It was a simple gesture, but it carried immense weight. At that moment, Emily realized she wasn't alone. She didn't have to carry everything by herself. The community was there to hold her, to lift her up when she needed it.

Personal Reflections on Connection

I began to see how much the community had shaped my own journey. The women who came to the ranch, the friends who supported me, and the horses who taught me about connection—all of them were part of my herd, my circle of trust.

Community wasn't just about being with others. It was about creating a space where everyone felt safe to be themselves, where vulnerability was met with compassion, where differences were celebrated rather than judged. It was about building relationships that nourished the soul and reminded me of the interconnectedness of all things.

One memory stood out. During a particularly difficult season in my life, I had been working with Gino, a gelding who carried his own scars from abandonment and rejection. Gino had taken months to trust me, but his eventual willingness to connect had mirrored my own growing openness to those around me. The patience I showed him and the trust he placed in me became a foundation for how I approached my human relationships.

Now, when I reflect on the journey of freedom and healing, I no longer see it as something to be achieved in solitude. The horses had shown me that strength wasn't about independence—it was about interdependence. It was about knowing when to stand alone and when to lean on those who walked the path beside me.

I had found my herd. And in that, I had found a deeper kind of freedom.

Action Steps for Chapter 14: The Role of Community

In this chapter, we explore the profound impact of community on healing, growth, and connection. These action steps will help you recognize, nurture, and engage with the communities in your life to support your journey toward freedom.

Action Step 1: Identifying Your Communities

- Make a list of the communities you are currently part of.
  - These might include family, friends, work groups, hobby or interest groups, spiritual communities, or any other circles.

- For each community, reflect:
  - What do I give to this community?

- o What does this community give to me?
- o Does this community align with my values and goals?

Action Step 2: Building Authentic Connections

- Choose one person in your community with whom you would like to deepen your connection.
  - o Schedule time for a meaningful conversation, coffee, or shared activity.

- During your time together:
  - o Share something vulnerable or significant about your life.
  - o Practice active listening, giving your full attention to their words and emotions.

Action Step 3: Reflecting on the Role of Horses

- Think about how the herd dynamics of horses reflect the role of community in your life.
  - o Who are the "grounded leaders" in your circle, providing stability and guidance?
  - o Who brings lightness and joy?
  - o Who challenges you to grow?

- Write a journal entry about how your community mirrors a herd and what roles you and others play.

Action Step 4: Strengthening Your Herd

- Identify areas in your community where you feel a need for more support or connection.
  - o What kind of people or relationships would fill this gap?
  - o How can you take steps to create or join a group that provides this support?

- Make an intentional effort to engage with this group or seek out new connections that align with your needs.

Action Step 5: Practicing Vulnerability

- Reflect on moments when you've hesitated to share your struggles or ask for help.
  - o What held you back?
  - o What might have been different if you had reached out?

- Choose one current challenge and share it with a trusted member of your community.
  - o Notice how sharing impacts your sense of connection and support.

Action Step 6: Giving Back

- Consider ways you can contribute to your community in meaningful ways.
  - o Could you offer support, share your knowledge, or simply be present for someone who needs it?

- Choose one act of kindness or service to give to your community this week.

Action Step 7: Gratitude for Your Herd

- Write a letter of gratitude to your community, or a specific person within it, acknowledging their impact on your life.
  - o You don't have to send the letter, but if you feel moved to share it, doing so can deepen your connection.

- End your letter with an affirmation: "I am grateful for the role this community plays in my life, and I am committed to nurturing these connections."

Integrating Chapter 14

The role of the community is essential in fostering connection, healing, and growth. By understanding the dynamics of your "herd" and intentionally engaging with it, you create a foundation of support and belonging.

CHAPTER 15

The Mirror Effect

The first time I fully grasped the concept of horses as mirrors was during a horsemanship clinic with a woman named Karen and her horse, Scooter. Scooter was a striking chestnut with a bold streak of independence that often bordered on defiance. Karen had described him as "impossible," a horse who wouldn't stand still, resisted being haltered, and seemed to test her at every turn.

Karen arrived at the clinic frustrated and unsure, her confidence worn thin from repeated struggles with Scooter. As the clinic began, she worked with him in the round pen under my guidance, but it quickly became clear that Scooter wasn't the only one struggling. Karen's movements were hesitant, her commands inconsistent. Scooter responded with resistance—ignoring her cues, pulling away, and refusing to engage.

Watching them, it became clear: Scooter wasn't being difficult for the sake of it. He was reflecting Karen's energy—her doubt, her lack of boundaries, her uncertainty. He wasn't the problem. He was the mirror.

Reflecting the Truth

That realization was a breakthrough for Karen and a profound reminder for me. Horses, I had learned, didn't lie. They didn't mask their emotions or pretend to be something they weren't. They lived fully in the moment, responding honestly to the energy presented to them.

As Karen worked with Scooter, she began to see her own patterns reflected in his behavior. When her movements became rushed or forceful, Scooter pulled away. When her cues were clear and her energy calm, Scooter softened. It wasn't about dominance or control—it was about connection.

The mirror effect wasn't always easy to face. It required participants to confront parts of themselves they had long ignored—doubts, fears, or insecurities. The lessons, however, paralleled my earlier realizations about breaking cycles (Chapter 13) and building trust within a community (Chapter 14). The mirror effect, I realized, was another layer of understanding myself through connection.

Tina and Saturn: A Lesson in Patience

Tina and Saturn presented a very different challenge. They had been together for six months, and instead of growing closer, their relationship seemed to be deteriorating. Saturn was becoming less confident, more resistant to being caught, and increasingly nervous during saddling and groundwork. By the time Tina climbed into the saddle, Saturn often seemed poised to either freeze or bolt at the slightest change in his environment.

Tina, frustrated and angry, described her horse as stubborn and resistant. But as I observed their routine, the truth became clear: Tina was task-oriented and barely noticed Saturn's escalating tension. Her rushed, abrupt movements and high expectations created an environment of pressure and urgency. Saturn, overwhelmed and anxious, responded with erratic and panicked behavior.

Rather than pausing to notice Saturn's reactions, Tina would scold him and become more forceful. She expected compliance, but her lack of presence and connection only fueled Saturn's insecurity.

When I encouraged Tina to pause and reflect, she recognized that her urgency and frustration were external expressions of her inner state. She wanted results without building trust, and Saturn was reflecting that impatience back to her. It wasn't easy for Tina to slow down and prioritize connection over outcome, but when she did, Saturn began to relax and respond. The process required patience, persistence, and humility, but the shift in their relationship was undeniable.

Growth Through Vulnerability

The mirror effect was a lesson I saw time and time again in my clinics. Women arrived with stories of fear, frustration, and a longing for connection with their horses. Many of them lacked the confidence to lead, unsure of how to set boundaries or communicate effectively.

One participant, Lisa, shared how her horse, Finn, constantly invaded her space. "He doesn't respect me," she said, exasperated. But as we worked together, it became evident that Lisa struggled to set boundaries—not just with Finn, but in her own life. She hesitated, second-guessed herself, and softened her energy at the wrong moments.

Under my guidance, Lisa learned to ground herself, to take up space, to project confidence. The transformation was immediate. Finn, once pushy and inattentive, began to mirror Lisa's newfound clarity and focus. By the end of the clinic, Lisa and Finn moved together in harmony, their connection strengthened by Lisa's willingness to address her own patterns.

Lessons in Reflection

My own experiences with the horses had taught me the same lessons. There was the time Rocky, my Gypsy Vanner, refused to follow my lead during a groundwork session. I had entered the pen distracted, my mind racing with worries about my workload. Rocky had picked up on my scattered energy and mirrored it back with resistance.

When I paused, took a breath, and approached him with clarity, Rocky responded immediately. His trust wasn't conditional—it was honest, a reflection of the energy I brought into the space. This echoed my earlier realization about how community and cycles shaped my relationships. The horses' honesty reinforced the interconnectedness I was beginning to embrace.

The mirror effect extended far beyond the round pen. It shaped how I viewed my relationships with people, my approach to challenges, and my understanding of myself.

Embracing the Reflection

The lessons of the mirror effect were humbling but invaluable. They taught me and the women I worked with that growth wasn't about fixing the horse—it was about looking inward. It was about recognizing the energy we brought into each interaction and having the courage to adjust when necessary.

One evening, after a particularly powerful clinic, I sat with my journal and wrote:

"The mirror effect is one of the greatest gifts the horses give us. It's not always easy to look at our own reflection, but it's in that reflection that we find the truth. They don't show us what we want to see—they show us what we need to see. And in doing so, they give us the opportunity to grow."

The mirror effect wasn't just a lesson. It was a gift, one that illuminated the path forward for all who were willing to look.

Action Steps for Chapter 15: The Mirror Effect

This chapter focuses on the idea that horses, like people, reflect the energy and emotions we bring into our relationships. These action steps will help you recognize and respond to the mirrors in your life, fostering greater self-awareness and connection.

Action Step 1: Reflecting on Your Own Mirror

- Choose one relationship in your life where you often experience frustration, conflict, or disconnection.
  - What behaviors or patterns do you notice in this person?
  - How might these behaviors mirror something in you, such as your fears, doubts, or unmet needs?

- Journal about this reflection:
  - What is this person or situation teaching me about myself?
  - How can I approach this relationship with greater awareness and compassion?

Action Step 2: Observing Energy Dynamics

- Spend time with someone close to you, such as a friend, family member, or coworker. Pay attention to how your energy affects their responses.
  - Are they calm, anxious, defensive, or open?
  - How does your mood or behavior seem to influence theirs?

- Reflect on how adjusting your energy—becoming calmer, more present, or more intentional—might create a shift in the dynamic.

Action Step 3: Practicing Presence with Horses or Animals

- If you have access to a horse or another animal, spend time with them in a quiet, undemanding way.

- o Observe their behavior, body language, and energy without trying to change it.
- o Notice how your energy influences their response to you.

- Journal about the experience:
  - o What did the horse or other animal reflect back to you?
  - o How did your presence or emotional state affect their behavior?

Action Step 4: Creating Space for Awareness

- Practice a grounding exercise to increase self-awareness:
  - o Sit or stand quietly, focusing on your breath. Inhale deeply for a count of four, hold for a count of four, and exhale for a count of four.
  - o As you breathe, notice any tension in your body and consciously release it.

- Use this practice before interacting with someone or making a decision. Observe how it changes your mindset and the interaction that follows.

Action Step 5: Releasing Perfectionism

- Think of a situation where you've held yourself—or someone else—to unrealistic standards of perfection.
  - o What beliefs or fears are driving this expectation?
  - o How can you replace perfectionism with curiosity or compassion?

- Write an affirmation to remind yourself: "I release the need for perfection. I trust the process of learning and growth, both in myself and others."

Action Step 6: Acknowledging Resistance

- Reflect on a time when you or someone in your life resisted change or growth.
  - o What fears or uncertainties might have caused this resistance?
  - o How could you have responded with greater patience or understanding?

- Practice recognizing resistance as a signal, not a problem. Ask: *What does this resistance want me to understand?*

Action Step 7: Celebrating Progress

- Identify one small moment of growth or connection—either with a person, a horse, or yourself—that you've experienced recently.
  - o What did this moment teach you about the mirror effect?
  - o How can you celebrate this progress, no matter how small?

- Write a note of gratitude to yourself or the person (or horse!) involved in this moment, acknowledging the value of their reflection in your life.

Integrating Chapter 15

The mirror effect is a powerful tool for self-awareness and growth. By observing and responding to the reflections in your relationships, you can deepen your understanding of yourself and create more meaningful connections.

CHAPTER 16

Expanding the Dream

Freedom brought not only clarity but also the courage to dream beyond the limits of what once seemed impossible. For years, my work had centered on helping women reconnect with their horses—and themselves. Through clinics, mentorships, and online programs, I had witnessed extraordinary transformations: women overcoming fear, learning to lead with confidence, and building bonds with their horses rooted in trust and understanding.

Now, standing on the foundation of my own growth, I began to imagine a future that extended far beyond my ranch. I could see the potential to impact more lives, create new opportunities, and deepen the reach of my work in ways that once felt out of reach. Reflecting on how fear had once held me back (Chapter 13) and how the power of community (Chapter 14) had propelled me forward, I realized this moment was the culmination of everything I had learned.

A Vision Born in the Pasture

The first seeds of this expansion were planted during a quiet morning in the pasture. I had been watching the horses graze, their movements slow and deliberate, when the thought came to me: *This is only the beginning.*

The realization both thrilled and unsettled me. For so long, I had kept my work contained, focused on the individual women and horses I worked with directly. It was safe, manageable, and familiar. But the more I leaned into my freedom, the more I felt the pull to explore new possibilities. There were stories to tell, lessons to share, and lives to touch. While I didn't yet know the full shape of what lay ahead, I felt drawn to something greater.

My horses had always shown me the way forward, and this moment was no different. Watching Harry, the ever-resilient ambassador of hope, graze alongside Dakota, the matriarch who led with quiet strength, I realized that my dream wasn't just about me. It was about the ripple effect of our collective lessons—the stories these horses carried and the lives they touched.

Transformative Clinics

One of the first ways this expansion began to take form was in my clinics. What had once been straightforward horsemanship lessons were evolving into transformative experiences for both the women and their horses. I designed exercises that challenged participants to confront their own limitations, step out of their comfort zones, and communicate with their horses in new ways.

At one clinic, a participant named Olivia worked with her mare, Honey, a palomino known for her stubborn streak. Olivia struggled with setting boundaries, both with Honey and in her own life. As they worked together, it became clear that Honey wasn't being difficult—she was testing Olivia's leadership.

"You can't just hope Honey will follow," I said, stepping into the arena to observe. "You need to lead with clarity and conviction. She's looking to you for direction, but first, you have to trust yourself."

Through a series of exercises, Olivia learned how to project confidence, even when she felt uncertain. By the end of the clinic, Honey was responding with a willingness and ease that reflected the shift in Olivia's energy. Months later, Olivia wrote to share how this confidence had transformed not just her relationship with Honey, but her approach to setting boundaries at work and in her family.

Moments like these reminded me why I had chosen this path: empowering women to become better leaders, not just for their horses but for themselves.

Reaching Beyond the Ranch

The dream expanded beyond the clinics. I began to imagine ways to reach women who couldn't attend in person. Online programs became an integral part of my work, offering lessons in leadership, confidence, and connection that transcended physical distance. I created videos and interactive exercises that taught participants to view their horse's behavior not as defiance but as communication.

"Horses aren't being bad to be bad," I said in one video. "They're trying to tell us something. Our job is to listen, adjust, and meet them where they are."

The feedback was overwhelming. Women from all over the world wrote to share how these lessons had transformed their relationships with their horses—and themselves. One participant, Maria, shared how understanding this principle helped her navigate challenges with her gelding, Ace. "For years, I thought Ace was stubborn," Maria wrote. "But now I realize he was trying to show me his fear. Once I started listening, everything changed."

Mentorship and Leadership

My one-on-one mentorship program also became a cornerstone of my work. Working closely with women and their horses, I saw how addressing a horse's challenges often required the owner to confront her own fears and beliefs. One mentee, Leah, struggled with her horse, Jasper, a high-energy gelding who frequently tested boundaries. Leah's hesitancy to enforce leadership stemmed from a lifelong fear of conflict.

"Jasper isn't challenging you because he's difficult," I told Leah during one session. "He's reflecting your uncertainty. He needs you to step into your role as a leader—not by being forceful, but by being clear."

Over time, Leah learned to lead with confidence, and Jasper responded with newfound respect and trust. Leah's journey extended far beyond the barn, as she began to set boundaries and assert herself in other areas of her life.

A Ripple Effect of Growth

As I reflected on these experiences, I began to see my work's ripple effect. The lessons I taught in clinics and mentorships didn't just impact the women in front of me; they extended to families, communities, and beyond. This realization inspired me to explore new ways to share my message with wider audiences.

Public speaking, once a daunting prospect, became an exciting challenge. My first engagement was at a local event, where I spoke about the lessons I had learned from the horses: the power of presence, the importance of trust, and the courage to lead. As I shared stories of women like Olivia, Maria, and Leah, I saw the audience light up with recognition.

One attendee approached me afterward, tears in her eyes. "You've changed the way I see my horse—and myself," she said. "Thank you."

Moments like these reinforced my commitment to sharing my work on a larger scale.

Building the Future

The conversations on the porch with my husband often turned to my dreams for the future. I talked about expanding my programs, collaborating with like-minded trainers and coaches, and building a legacy that would continue to touch lives long after my time. He listened patiently, then said, "You've always had this in you. It's just taken you a while to see it."

His words stayed with me. The dream wasn't something new—it was the natural progression of everything I had built. It was the next step on a path I had been walking all along.

Reflection and Action Steps

As I journaled that evening, I wrote:

"Growth isn't about chasing something bigger—it's about stepping fully into who you are. It's about trusting that your work, your story, and your life have value. It's about embracing the unknown and leading with courage, knowing that every step forward brings you closer to the impact you're meant to make."

The horizon stretched before me, vast and full of promise. And for the first time, I felt not just ready but eager to explore where it would lead.

Action Steps for Chapter 16: Expanding the Dream

In this chapter, the focus shifts to embracing the vision of what's possible and stepping into a life guided by authenticity and courage. The following action steps are designed to help you expand your dreams while staying aligned with your values and purpose.

Action Step 1: Clarify Your Vision

- Take a quiet moment to reflect on your dreams and goals. Ask yourself:
  - What is calling to me right now?
  - If I could achieve or create anything without fear of failure, what would it be?

- Write down your vision in as much detail as possible:
  - Include what it looks like, feels like, and how it aligns with your values.
  - Don't censor yourself—let your imagination flow.

Action Step 2: Break It Into Steps

- Take one part of your vision—something that feels meaningful yet achievable—and break it down into smaller steps.
  - Example: If your dream is to connect with others through teaching, your first step might be to outline a class or workshop idea.

- Write down the first three steps you can take today, no matter how small:
  - Step 1: _____
  - Step 2: _____
  - Step 3: _____

Action Step 3: Reflect on Alignment

- Reflect on how your dream aligns with your core values:
  - Does this vision feel authentic and true to who I am?
  - How will pursuing this dream contribute to my sense of purpose and fulfillment?

- Adjust your vision if needed to ensure it reflects your heart, not external expectations.

Action Step 4: Address Fear and Doubt

- Write down any fears or doubts that come up as you think about expanding your dream.
  - Example: "What if I fail?" or "I'm not good enough to do this."

- Respond to each fear with compassion and curiosity:
  - What is this fear trying to protect me from?
  - How can I reframe this fear as an opportunity for growth?

Action Step 5: Share Your Dream

- Share your vision with someone you trust—a friend, mentor, or partner—who can encourage and support you.
  - Explain why this dream matters to you and what you're doing to make it happen.

- Notice how speaking your dream aloud deepens your commitment to it.

Action Step 6: Create Space for Expansion

- Carve out dedicated time each week to work on your dream, even if it's just 30 minutes.
  - Use this time to brainstorm, research, or take actionable steps toward your goal.

- Treat this time as sacred—honor it as an investment in your future.

Action Step 7: Celebrate Small Wins

- Reflect on any progress you've made toward your dream, no matter how small.
    - o Did you take a step outside your comfort zone? Did you learn something new? Celebrate it!

- Write down one thing you're proud of today and how it brings you closer to your vision.

Integrating Chapter 16

Expanding your dream is about courage, clarity, and alignment. These action steps will help you take meaningful strides toward your vision while staying connected to your purpose and values.

CHAPTER 17

Living in Alignment

Living in alignment wasn't a single choice or a moment of clarity—it was an ongoing practice, a commitment I made every day to honor my values, trust my intuition, and stay true to my path. It was about weaving together all the parts of myself—the beautiful woman, the inner child, the fearless teacher, and the vulnerable seeker—and allowing them to exist in harmony. It was also about partnership, not only with the women and horses I worked with but with myself. Alignment wasn't about striving for perfection; it was about showing up authentically, moment by moment.

Finding Flow in Nature

One morning, as I walked through the pasture, the sun rising softly over the hills, I reflected on what alignment truly meant. The horses moved gracefully around me, their movements fluid and instinctive. They didn't carry the weight of self-doubt or overthink their actions. They lived fully in the present, responding to their environment with an intuitive wisdom that I deeply admired.

I thought of Apache, who always seemed to find balance within the herd no matter how the dynamics shifted. Apache didn't force connection or control his surroundings; he simply existed in a way that inspired trust and respect. Watching him, I realized that living in alignment meant finding that same sense of flow within myself. It meant moving through life with authenticity and presence, trusting that everything I needed was already within me.

But alignment, for me, required intentionality. Unlike the horses, I had spent much of my life disconnected—from myself, from my body, from the inner voice that guided me. To live in alignment, I had to learn to listen again—to my heart, my intuition, and the subtle messages of my nervous system. I had to learn to trust myself.

Reevaluating Priorities

One of the first steps was reevaluating how I spent my time. I had always been a doer, packing my days with tasks and responsibilities. But this constant busyness had often come at the expense of my well-being. Living in alignment meant letting go of the need to prove myself through productivity. It meant creating space for what truly mattered.

I began my mornings with intentional stillness, journaling my thoughts or simply sitting quietly in the pasture. I carved out time to be with the horses, not for training or work but to simply connect. I gave myself permission to rest, to laugh, to play. And I started saying no—to projects, to obligations, to anything that didn't align with my values.

These changes didn't happen overnight. There were days when old habits crept back in, when the voice of self-doubt whispered that I wasn't doing enough. But I met those moments with compassion, reminding myself that alignment wasn't about doing more—it was about doing what felt right.

Lessons from Horses and People

The lessons from the horses continued to guide me. During a horsemanship clinic, I worked with a woman named Anna and her mare, Stormy. Anna had come to the clinic hoping to rebuild her confidence after a frightening fall. Stormy, a spirited gray mare, mirrored Anna's hesitation, her movements tense and uncertain.

As we worked together, I encouraged Anna to focus on her energy, to let go of the need to control Stormy, and instead connect with her. "She's not trying to test you," I explained. "She's communicating. She's asking if she can trust you to lead her. That trust starts with you."

It was a powerful moment. Anna began to soften, her body language shifting as she breathed deeply and let herself be present. Stormy responded almost immediately, lowering her head and moving closer. By the end of the session, they were navigating the obstacle course together, their movements in sync. The transformation wasn't just in Stormy—it was in Anna, who had found a piece of her own alignment through the process.

Letting Go of Control

One evening, I thought back to a session with Luna, a young mare who had challenged my patience and expectations. Luna had been hesitant and guarded, resisting every attempt to move forward. Frustrated, I had stepped back, unsure of what else to do. And then it hit me: I didn't need to do anything. I just needed to be present.

I let go of my need for progress and stood quietly, offering Luna the space to make her own decision. Slowly, the mare began to move toward me, her eyes softening with trust. The moment was a reminder that alignment wasn't about forcing outcomes. It was about trusting the process, about meeting myself and others where we were.

Embracing Imperfection

Living in alignment also meant embracing my own humanity. I wasn't perfect, and I didn't need to be. There were days when I felt uncertain or overwhelmed, when fear or doubt crept in. But instead of judging myself, I met those moments with grace.

As I shared these lessons in my clinics and programs, I noticed how much they resonated with the women I worked with. They, too, were learning to navigate their fears, to trust their instincts, to lead their horses—and their lives—with authenticity. One participant, a woman named Rachel, described how her work with her gelding, Tucker, had changed since the clinic. "I realized I was so focused on doing everything right that I wasn't even seeing him," Rachel said. "When I started paying attention to his cues, everything shifted. It's like we're finally on the same page."

Hearing stories like Rachel's filled me with a deep sense of purpose. I wasn't just teaching horsemanship; I was teaching alignment—how to listen, how to connect, how to lead with integrity.

Reflection and Commitment

That evening, as I wrote in my journal, I reflected on what living in alignment had taught me:

"Alignment isn't about getting it right every time. It's about showing up as yourself, fully and honestly. It's about listening to your heart, trusting your intuition, and honoring the truth of who you are. And it's about creating a ripple effect, inspiring others to find their own alignment by living yours."

The journey wasn't over. Alignment wasn't a destination; it was a practice, something I would choose every day. But as I looked out at the horizon, I felt a deep sense of peace. I was exactly where I was meant to be, walking my path with clarity and courage. And in that alignment, I found my freedom.

Action Steps for Chapter 17: Living in Alignment

In this chapter, the emphasis is on the practice of living in alignment—being true to your values, intuition, and authentic self. The following action steps will help you cultivate alignment in your daily life and relationships.

Action Step 1: Define Your Core Values

- Reflect on what truly matters to you.
  - Ask yourself: *What are the non-negotiable values that guide my life?* (e.g., honesty, kindness, growth, connection)

- Write down your top three to five core values:
  - Value 1: _____
  - Value 2: _____
  - Value 3: _____

Action Step 2: Conduct a Life Alignment Check

- Evaluate the different areas of your life—relationships, career, personal growth, health, etc.
  - Are your actions and choices in these areas aligned with your core values?
  - Where do you feel the most alignment? Where do you feel misaligned?

- Identify one area where you'd like to bring more alignment:
  - Area to focus on: _____

Action Step 3: Reconnect with Your Inner Voice

- Take five to ten minutes each day to sit quietly and tune in to your intuition. Ask yourself:
  - What is my heart telling me today?

- What do I need most at this moment?

- Write down any insights or feelings that arise.

Action Step 4: Set Daily Intentions

- Each morning, set a simple intention that aligns with your values and priorities.
  - Example: "Today, I will approach my work with curiosity and compassion."

- Reflect on your intention at the end of the day. Did it guide your actions? How did it feel?

Action Step 5: Practice Saying No

- Identify situations where you've said yes to something that didn't align with your values or priorities.
- Practice setting boundaries by saying no when something doesn't feel aligned:
  - Example: "Thank you for the opportunity, but I need to prioritize my current commitments."

Action Step 6: Align Your Energy

- Notice how your energy shifts throughout the day. Ask yourself:
  - When do I feel most alive and connected to my values?
  - When do I feel drained or disconnected?

- Adjust your schedule, environment, or activities to better align with what energizes you.

Action Step 7: Celebrate Moments of Alignment

- Reflect on a recent moment when you felt deeply aligned with your values and authentic self.
    - What made that moment meaningful?
    - How can you create more moments like it?

- Write down three ways you will honor and celebrate alignment in your life this week.

Integrating Chapter 17

Living in alignment is a daily practice, not a destination. These steps are designed to help you reconnect with your inner truth, make choices that honor your values, and create a life that feels authentic and meaningful.

CHAPTER 18

The Woman and the Inner Child

I had walked out of the prison of my mind hand in hand with the beautiful woman and the inner child. Our steps had been tentative at first, the embers of the fire still smoldering behind us. But as we moved forward together, I began to realize the depth of this reunion. The beautiful woman—my authentic self—was the fullest expression of who I had always been meant to be. The inner child, tender and vulnerable, carried the wonder and innocence that had been locked away by shame, fear, and guilt. Now, we were all learning to coexist, not as separate parts but as an integrated whole.

It wasn't a simple process. Each part of me had its own needs, its own voice, its own fears and strengths. The inner child was curious and playful but also hesitant, quick to retreat at the first sign of discomfort. The beautiful woman radiated strength and wisdom but was still learning to step fully into the light. And I—caught between the two—was figuring out how to weave them together into a life of alignment and wholeness.

Learning to Listen

The first challenge was learning to listen. For years, I had silenced the voices within me—the inner child's cries for safety and the beautiful woman's call to authenticity. Now, as we began to walk together, I realized how much they had to teach me.

The inner child spoke in moments of vulnerability, bringing forth memories and emotions I had long buried. One evening, as I sat journaling, the child's voice rose within me: "Why did you leave me? Why didn't you protect me?"

My heart ached at the question, tears spilling onto the page. "I'm sorry," I whispered aloud. "I thought I was keeping you safe by hiding you away. I didn't know how to protect you. But I see you now, and I won't leave you again."

The beautiful woman, on the other hand, guided me with quiet strength. She was the part of me that had always known the truth—that I was worthy, capable, and enough. The woman didn't speak in words so much as in a feeling, a calm certainty that settled in my chest when I made choices aligned with my values. Together, they helped me navigate the journey, each offering something essential.

The Mirror of the Herd

I saw this dynamic reflected in the horses. They, too, embodied a balance of strength and vulnerability, of instinct and wisdom. The herd thrived on connection, each horse playing a role in the group's harmony. Watching them, I began to see my own internal dynamic more clearly.

One afternoon, I worked with a mare named Grace, who had a habit of freezing when asked to step into new situations. Grace reminded me of the inner child—cautious, hesitant, and quick to retreat when she felt unsafe. Instead of pushing Grace forward, I paused, softening my energy and waiting. Slowly, the mare began to relax, her ears flicking toward me, her breathing deepening.

"That's it," I said quietly, my voice steady. "Take your time. We're in this together."

As Grace took a tentative step forward, I felt a shift within myself. It wasn't just the mare learning to trust—it was my inner child, mirroring the process of finding safety and courage. I thought back to lessons from earlier journeys, like learning to trust myself in Chapter 13, and realized how they had built the foundation for this moment.

Navigating the Journey

The journey wasn't linear. There were moments of progress when the inner child laughed and danced in the sunlight, and the beautiful woman stood tall, guiding me forward with grace. But there were also moments when old fears surfaced, pulling us back into the shadows.

During one clinic, a participant named Heather struggled with a reactive gelding named Clyde. Heather's frustration grew as Clyde balked at every cue, his body tense and unyielding.

"He's not being difficult to test you," I told Heather gently. "He's asking for clarity. He needs to know you're here, that you're leading with trust."

As Heather softened her approach, Jasper began to mirror her calmness, his resistance melting into connection. Watching them, I thought of the inner child—how my own hesitations weren't signs of defiance but calls for reassurance. Leading myself, like leading a horse, required patience, presence, and unwavering trust.

Integration and Wholeness

As the days turned into weeks, I began to feel the pieces of myself coming together. The inner child, once hidden and afraid, now walked beside me, bringing a sense of wonder and curiosity. The beautiful woman, once stifled by fear and shame, now guided me with strength and wisdom. And I, the storyteller of this journey, was learning to live in alignment with them both.

In my journal, I wrote:

"The woman and the inner child are not separate from me. They are me—two essential parts of the whole. The child reminds me to stay curious and open. The woman shows me how to live with courage and authenticity. Together, we are strong. Together, we are free."

One evening, as I stood in the pasture, watching the sunset paint the sky in hues of gold and crimson, I felt a deep sense of peace. The beautiful woman stood beside me, radiating quiet confidence. The inner child reached for my hand, her eyes wide with wonder.

"We've come so far," I said softly, my voice steady. "And we're just getting started."

The inner child smiled, her face alight with joy. "I knew you'd find me," she said. "I was waiting for you."

I knelt down, wrapping the child in a gentle embrace. "I'm glad I did," I whispered. "I'm glad we're here—together."

Wholeness in Action

The horses continued to mirror our journey, their presence a constant reminder of what it meant to live authentically. Each day brought new lessons, new challenges, and new opportunities to grow. And through it all, I carried the voices of the inner child and the beautiful woman within me, each guiding me in their own way.

Living in alignment with all parts of myself wasn't easy, but it was worth it. It was the path to freedom, to wholeness, to becoming the person I was always meant to be. The foundations of community and connection from Chapter 14 and the trust built in Chapter 15 were now fully integrated into my daily life.

And in that integration, I found my strength, my peace, and my truth.

Action Steps for Chapter 18: The Woman and the Inner Child

In this chapter, we explore the relationship between the woman and the inner child—two vital aspects of your authentic self. These action steps are designed to help you connect with and nurture your inner child while integrating her with your adult self.

Action Step 1: Meet Your Inner Child

- Set aside a quiet moment and imagine your inner child sitting beside you.
  - Visualize her: What does she look like? How old is she? What emotions does she carry?
  - If visualization feels difficult, write about her instead. Describe her personality, fears, and joys.

- Write a letter to your inner child. Begin with:
- "Dear Inner Child, I see you, and I want you to know..."

Action Step 2: Create a Safe Space

- Reflect on what safety feels like for you and your inner child. Ask:
  - What makes me feel safe and supported?
  - What would make my inner child feel secure and loved?

- Create a ritual or physical space that feels comforting, such as lighting a candle, sitting with a favorite blanket, or journaling in a special notebook.

Action Step 3: Listen to Her Needs

- Take a moment each day to check in with your inner child:
  - Ask: "What do you need from me today?" or "What would make you happy?"

- Write down her responses or any emotions that arise, even if they feel unclear or unexpected.

Action Step 4: Reparent Yourself

- Identify an area where your inner child may feel unsupported (e.g., fear of making mistakes, need for validation, or feeling unseen).
- Write a supportive response as the wise, compassionate adult:
  - Example: "It's okay to make mistakes. They're part of learning, and I'll always be here to guide you."

- Practice giving yourself the care and reassurance you may have needed as a child.

Action Step 5: Engage in Play

- Find an activity that your inner child would enjoy, such as drawing, dancing, or playing outside.
- Let go of perfection and judgment. Focus on having fun and being present in the moment.
  - Ask: *What did I love doing as a child?* Revisit one of those activities this week.

Action Step 6: Rewrite a Story

- Reflect on a memory where your inner child felt unseen, unsupported, or hurt.
  - o Write about the memory as it happened.
  - o Then rewrite it, imagining the compassionate adult version of yourself stepping in to support and comfort her.

- Reflect on how this shift in perspective changes the way you feel about that memory.

Action Step 7: Celebrate Wholeness

- Write down three ways the woman and the inner child work together to make you whole:
  - o Example: "The inner child brings joy and curiosity, and the woman provides wisdom and strength."

- Reflect on a recent moment where you felt the two aspects of yourself working in harmony. Celebrate that connection.

Integrating Chapter 18

The relationship between the woman and the inner child is an ongoing journey. These steps will help you nurture that connection, creating a foundation of trust, love, and wholeness that supports every aspect of your life.

CHAPTER 19

The Legacy of Freedom

Freedom wasn't just a gift I had reclaimed—it was a legacy I was living and offering to others. My transformation was no longer contained within the boundaries of my ranch or my journal; it rippled outward, touching lives, inspiring change, and reminding others of what was possible. Freedom, I realized, was the seed of a legacy that could take root in the hearts of everyone it touched.

The foundation of this legacy had been laid through my personal journey—the courage to walk away from the prison of my mind, the rediscovery of the inner child, and the emergence of the beautiful woman within me. These once-fractured parts of myself had come together, weaving a tapestry of authenticity and strength that I now carried into every facet of my work. This integration gave me the clarity and confidence to lead others toward their own transformations.

Planting the Seeds of Change

The legacy began with the women who came to my clinics and mentorship programs, many of them carrying invisible burdens. They arrived with stories of fear, longing, and self-doubt, seeking clarity, connection, and a way back to themselves. They didn't come just to learn about horses—they came to rediscover their own power.

One of those women was Debbie, a mother of three who had spent years pouring her energy into everyone but herself. Debbie brought her horse, Charlie, to a clinic, describing him as unpredictable and aloof. As they worked together, Debbie began to see that her horse's behavior was mirroring her own exhaustion and disconnection.

At one point, during a simple groundwork exercise, Charlie stopped and resisted moving forward. Debbie's body stiffened as frustration and tension radiated through her posture. Her shoulders pulled back tightly, and her breathing became shallow.

"Why won't he just listen?" Debbie asked, her voice tinged with exasperation.

I approached calmly, standing beside her with a quiet confidence. "Charlie isn't ignoring you," I said gently. "He's communicating. He's asking you to show up—not perfectly, but with clarity and presence. Can you let go of what's holding you back and give him that?"

Debbie exhaled slowly, consciously softening her body. Her movements became more deliberate, her energy calmer. When she asked Charlie to move forward again, he responded, matching her steps as though they had found a rhythm together. The transformation wasn't just in the horse—it was in Debbie, too.

By the end of the clinic, Debbie had begun to find that presence not just with her horse but within herself. She wasn't "fixed"—healing didn't work that way—but she had found a starting point, a spark of possibility.

A Collaborative Legacy

My work with the horses became the foundation of my legacy. Each horse carried its own lessons. Daisy, the skittish mare, taught the patience required to build trust. Rocky, the steadfast Gypsy Vanner, embodied grounded leadership, while Katniss, the curious filly, celebrated the joy of embracing the unknown. These horses weren't just participants—they were collaborators, their honest and reflective nature creating a space for transformation that no human could replicate. They formed the heart of the legacy, grounding and inspiring all who encountered them.

Expanding the Reach

My legacy extended beyond the clinics and mentorship programs. Messages began arriving from women I had never met in person but whose lives had been touched by my story.

One wrote, "Hearing about your journey helped me recognize the patterns I've been stuck in for years. I'm finally giving myself permission to change."

Another shared, "I've always been afraid of failing, but you've shown me that mistakes are part of growth. Thank you for helping me find the courage to try."

Each message was a reminder of the power of sharing my truth, of creating space for others to step into their own freedom. The impact wasn't confined to the ranch—it was rippling out into the world, reaching people I might never meet but whose lives were connected to mine in unseen ways.

My dream crystallized into a vision for a sanctuary—a haven where horses and humans could heal and grow together. I saw mustangs transitioning from the wild into lives defined by trust and partnership, their stories mirroring the resilience of the women they touched. Beyond the sanctuary, I imagined training a network of facilitators who would carry this work into new communities, weaving a global tapestry of equine wisdom and human transformation.

Navigating Overwhelm with Grace

The possibilities were vast, and at times they felt overwhelming. One evening, as I reviewed plans for expanding the clinics while fielding questions from my growing network, doubt crept in. *Could I balance my vision with the realities of time, resources, and energy?* The scope of my dream often felt too big, but I reminded myself that every great journey began with a single step.

Whenever doubt crept in, I leaned on the inner child and the beautiful woman within me. The child reminded me to stay curious, to embrace the wonder of possibility. The woman, steady and wise, grounded me, whispering, "You've got this. Just take the next step."

The horses mirrored this balance. Watching their calm presence in the pasture, I found reassurance in their simplicity. They didn't worry about the future—they lived fully in the present, trusting that the herd and the land would provide what they needed.

A Legacy in Action

One evening, as I stood at the fence watching the sun dip below the horizon, I thought about the word *legacy*. It wasn't about fame or recognition; it was about the lives I touched, the lessons I shared, the seeds I planted in the hearts of others. My legacy wasn't just mine—it belonged to the horses, the women, the community we had built together.

Pulling out my journal, I wrote:

"Legacy isn't what we leave behind—it's what we live every day. It's the way we show up, the love we give, the truths we share. It's the lives we touch and the freedom we inspire. My legacy is woven from the threads of every connection, every lesson, every moment of courage and grace. Together, we are creating something that will outlive us all."

As the stars began to emerge in the night sky, I felt a deep sense of peace. The legacy of freedom wasn't just a dream—it was already unfolding, one woman, one horse, one story at a time. And I knew, with every fiber of my being, that it would continue to grow.

Because freedom, when shared, is limitless. And the ripple of its impact is unstoppable.

Action Steps for Chapter 19: The Legacy of Freedom

This chapter explores the ripple effect of freedom and how sharing your journey can inspire and transform others. These action steps will guide you in living your legacy of freedom and amplifying its impact.

Action Step 1: Reflect on Your Legacy

- Take 10 minutes to journal on the following prompts:
  o What do I want to be remembered for?
  o What values guide the way I live and interact with others?
  o How am I already leaving a positive impact on those around me?

Action Step 2: Identify Your Ripple Effect

- Reflect on moments like Debbie's transformation with Charlie—times when your presence or insight created a spark of change in someone else's life.
- Write down three such moments, focusing on the authenticity and connection that made a difference. Let these reflections guide your understanding of the ripple effect of your legacy and inspire new ways to expand its reach.

Action Step 3: Share Your Story

- Identify a part of your journey that feels powerful or meaningful to share—whether it's a triumph, a challenge, or a lesson learned.
- Decide how you want to share it: through a conversation, a social media post, or even in a journal if you're not ready to share publicly.
  - Focus on authenticity rather than perfection.

Action Step 4: Practice Living Your Legacy Daily

- Choose one way to embody your values today, such as:
  - Offering encouragement to someone who needs it.
  - Practicing a moment of gratitude for your journey.
  - Taking a step toward a goal that reflects your personal freedom.

- Reflect on how these actions contribute to the legacy you're building.

Action Step 5: Connect Through Mentorship

- Consider ways you can support others in their own journeys:
  - Reach out to someone who might benefit from your encouragement or experience.
  - Offer to share a resource, lesson, or story that helped you grow.

- Write down how mentoring others aligns with your vision of freedom and legacy.

Action Step 6: Partner with Your Horses

- Spend time observing your horse or another animal in your life. Reflect on how their behaviors and responses mirror your energy and actions.
- Journal on the following:
  o What lessons has this horse taught me about connection, trust, or freedom?
  o How can I share these lessons with others in a meaningful way?

Action Step 7: Write Your Legacy Statement

- In one or two sentences, define your legacy. Focus on the essence of what you want to pass on to others.
  o Example: "My legacy is to inspire courage and authenticity, helping others find freedom by living in alignment with their true selves."

- Keep this statement somewhere visible to remind you of the impact you are creating.

Integrating Chapter 19

These steps encourage you to reflect on the legacy of freedom you are living and sharing. By embracing the ripple effect of your journey, you inspire transformation not only within yourself but also in the lives of those around you.

CHAPTER 20

A New Horizon

The horizon stretched wide before me, limitless and full of possibility. The journey I had undertaken—breaking free from old patterns, reclaiming my freedom, and deepening my connection to myself, the horses, and others—had brought me to a place of profound peace. This was the essence of home: not a physical location, but a state of being. Yet, as much as I felt at peace, I knew the journey wasn't over. This was only the beginning.

Freedom, I had learned, wasn't a one-time achievement. It was a practice, a daily commitment to live authentically, to trust myself, and to walk with courage into the unknown. The lessons I had absorbed from the horses, from the women I worked with, and from my own inner journey were not stagnant. They were alive, evolving, and calling me to new horizons.

A Life in Alignment

One crisp winter morning, as I walked among the horses, the air filled with the soft crunch of frost underfoot, I paused to watch the herd. They moved as one, fluid and attuned to one another. The simplicity of their connection reminded me of everything I had worked toward: alignment, presence, trust.

My vision for the future was taking shape. It wasn't about building something grand for the sake of ambition; it was about deepening my commitment to living and working in a way that felt true to my values.

I dreamed of creating a sanctuary that was as much for the people as it was for the horses—a place where both could find healing, connection, and freedom. I envisioned clinics that gave women not only the tools to communicate with their horses, but also the courage to step into their own power.

Within me, the beautiful woman and the inner child walked together, each lending something vital to this vision. The child reminded me of the joy in the unknown, the playful curiosity that made my dreams feel alive. The woman brought wisdom, focus, and an unwavering belief that the work was worth doing.

But most of all, I dreamed of continuing to live a life guided by integrity and heart. The work wasn't about me—it was about creating ripples, about helping others discover their own path to freedom. Every small act of transformation was another thread in the legacy I was weaving.

Lessons Passed On

The final clinic of the year brought women from all walks of life to the ranch. Some arrived with fear in their eyes, unsure if they were ready to face the challenges ahead. Others carried the weight of self-doubt, wondering if they were capable of creating the connection with their horses that they so deeply desired.

Over the course of the clinic, I saw transformation take root in the smallest, most meaningful ways. There was Rachel, whose gelding, Chance, had always bolted when faced with uncertainty. Rachel confessed that her own tendency was to freeze, to hesitate, and in her hesitation, Chance had learned to flee.

In the round pen, Rachel stood stiff with fear as Chance danced nervously along the perimeter. I watched as Rachel's body tensed, her shoulders rigid, her breathing shallow. Quietly, I stepped forward.

"Breathe," I said softly. "He's looking to you. Show him it's safe by being safe yourself."

Rachel took a breath—then another. Slowly, her body softened. Chance slowed his frantic pacing and turned to face her, his ears flicking forward. The connection was fragile at first, but it grew as Rachel let herself settle into the moment. By the end of the session, Chance stood calmly beside her, his trust reflected in her newfound calm.

"You taught him that," I said, smiling at Rachel. "Not by controlling him, but by leading him with your energy."

Moments like these reminded me why I did this work. The horses were the mirrors, the teachers, the partners in transformation. Through them, the women who came to my clinics found not just better relationships with their horses but deeper connections to themselves. They learned to listen, to trust, and to lead—not through force, but through presence and intention.

A Ripple Effect

My work extended far beyond the fences of the ranch. I began to hear from women who had participated in my clinics or read my writing, sharing the ripples that had spread into their own lives. They wrote about how they had carried the lessons into their relationships, their careers, and their families. They spoke of newfound confidence, of letting go of fear, of stepping into leadership—not just with their horses, but also with themselves.

My heart swelled with gratitude as I read their messages. One wrote, "Hearing about your journey helped me recognize the patterns I've been stuck in for years. I'm finally giving myself permission to change."

Another shared, "I've always been afraid of failing, but you've shown me that mistakes are part of growth. Thank you for helping me find the courage to try."

Each message reminded me of the profound impact of sharing my truth and creating space for others to step into their own freedom. The work wasn't confined to the ranch—it was reaching people I might never meet but whose lives were connected to mine in unseen ways. This ripple effect wasn't just evidence of my impact; it was my legacy in motion.

A Legacy of Freedom

The horizon was no longer a distant concept. It was alive in every life touched, every story shared, every moment of connection created. My legacy was not something I had to chase; it was something I lived every day. It was in the way I showed up for myself, for the horses, for the women who came to my ranch. It was in the lessons I passed on, the spaces I created for transformation, and the freedom I modeled through my own life.

My inner child marveled at the vastness of it all, her sense of wonder rekindled by the possibilities. The beautiful woman stood strong, guiding the way with clarity and purpose. Together, they carried the lessons of the past and the dreams of the future.

Preparing for the Next Chapter

As I stood at the edge of the pasture one evening, the winter sun dipping low in the sky, I thought about RC. The horse who had carried me through some of the darkest and most transformative moments of my life. His story wasn't just my story—it was the story of freedom, of connection, of everything this journey had been about.

I smiled, knowing it was time to share it in full. The story of RC wasn't just the epilogue to this book; it was the heart of my legacy, the bridge between where I had been and where I was going. It was the perfect way to close this chapter of my life and open the next.

Looking Ahead

The path ahead was open and full of possibility, and I was ready to walk it, with the lessons of the past as my foundation and the promise of the future as my guide. The horizon stretched wide, and as I stepped forward, I carried with me the unwavering belief that freedom was not a destination but a way of being.

I was free. I was whole. And I was ready for whatever came next.

Action Steps for Chapter 20: A New Horizon

This chapter invites you to embrace the limitless possibilities that come with freedom and alignment. These action steps will help you reflect on the lessons you've learned, set intentions for the future, and step confidently into the next phase of your journey.

Action Step 1: Visualize Your Horizon

- Find a quiet space and close your eyes. Take a few deep breaths and imagine the horizon of your life as it stretches out before you.
    - What does it look like? Feel like? What emotions arise?

- Write a description of this vision in your journal, focusing on the possibilities and opportunities you see.

Action Step 2: Set Your Intentions

- Reflect on the key themes of your journey so far. Ask yourself:
  - What do I want to carry forward from this experience?
  - What new opportunities or directions excite me?

- Write down three specific intentions for the next chapter of your life, ensuring they align with your values and authentic self.

Action Step 3: Anchor in Gratitude

- Write a list of everything you are grateful for on this journey, including lessons learned, connections made, and moments of growth.
  - Be specific—focus on people, experiences, or even challenges that have shaped you.

- Read this list aloud, allowing yourself to feel gratitude for how far you've come.

Action Step 4: Create a Freedom Map

- Draw or write a "map" that represents your path to freedom:
  - Include the major milestones, lessons, and transformations you've experienced.
  - Mark the current point on your map and label the horizon with your next goal or aspiration.

- Reflect on how this map tells the story of your journey and inspires your next steps.

Action Step 5: Practice Expanding Your Vision

- Spend 10 minutes each morning visualizing one small step toward your goals. Imagine yourself achieving it and how it feels.

- Take one action, no matter how small, that moves you closer to this vision. Track your progress in a journal.

Action Step 6: Share Your Journey

- Identify one person who could benefit from hearing your story of transformation and freedom.
- Share a part of your journey with them, focusing on the lessons that have made the most impact on your life.

Action Step 7: Partner with Your Horses

- Spend time with your horse or another animal that has been part of your journey. Reflect on how their presence has shaped your growth and vision.
- As you work with them, stay attuned to their responses and mirror their presence as a reminder of alignment and trust.

Action Step 8: Journal Your Future Story

- Imagine yourself one year from now, living fully in alignment and stepping boldly into your new horizon.
  - What are you doing? How do you feel? What impact are you making?
- Write this as though it has already happened, anchoring your vision in the present.

Integrating Chapter 20

These steps are designed to help you reflect on your journey, embrace the possibilities ahead, and step into your new horizon with courage and intention. By integrating these practices, you create the foundation for a life of ongoing growth, freedom, and connection.

RC's Legacy and Mine

Some stories linger long after they're told, weaving themselves into the very fabric of who we are. The story of RC and me is one such story—a story of love, loss, and the kind of transformation that only comes from walking through the fire.

I met RC as a yearling, a wild palomino saved from a PMU rescue in North Dakota. He was just a colt then, his future uncertain, but there was something about him—a spark, a depth—that spoke to me in a way no horse ever had. I brought him home, not knowing that he would become not just a partner but a mirror, a teacher, and a guide.

A Bond Forged Through Trials

RC and I spent over a decade together, sharing countless hours on trails, in arenas, and in the quiet moments that build unshakable trust. He taught me how to listen with my heart, to move with intention, and to communicate without words. Together, we danced to the unspoken rhythm of mutual respect and love.

But our bond wasn't without its trials. RC was my partner in some of the most challenging moments of my life. In forty years of working with horses, I've only been seriously injured three times—and all three involved RC. Those experiences weren't about blame or fault. They were the crucible in which our connection was forged, the moments that tested the strength of what we had built.

One such moment left me lying unconscious in a pasture with a triple brain bleed, still holding onto RC's halter. Another cost me a finger in a freak accident that shook the foundations of our relationship. These weren't just physical challenges—they were mirrors of my own inner fears and vulnerabilities. In those moments, RC became more than a horse. He became a reflection of my resilience and my capacity to heal.

The Abyss and the Light

After the accident that took my finger, I found myself lost—not just physically but emotionally. The connection I had with RC, once so vibrant, felt distant. I avoided him, unsure how to face the mix of fear, mistrust, and grief that had taken root in my heart. It wasn't just about RC—it was about me. I had to confront the pain I had long buried, the shame and guilt I carried, and the stories I told myself about worthiness and failure.

RC mirrored my journey. He, too, withdrew, becoming distant from the herd and hesitant to engage with me. It was as if he were waiting for me to return to myself before he could return to me. And so, I began the slow, uncomfortable process of healing—not by pushing the pain away but by leaning into it, by sitting with the discomfort and allowing it to teach me.

Joseph Campbell's words became a beacon during this time: "It is by going down into the abyss that we recover the treasures of life. Where you stumble, there lies your treasure."

RC became my treasure, the golden light in the darkness of my abyss. He taught me to trust again, not just in him but in myself. He showed me that healing is a partnership—that both horse and human carry the scars of trauma and that both must be given the space to heal. Through this journey, I found not just recovery but a renewed connection to RC and the courage to face what lay ahead.

The Hero's Journey

As I faced my fears, I discovered strengths I didn't know I had. I learned to sit with my vulnerability, to listen to the whispers of my heart, and to reconnect with the person I had always been beneath the layers of shame and doubt. And in doing so, I found my way back to RC, our bond deeper and more resilient than ever.

RC's lessons extended far beyond our partnership. He became a guiding force in how I worked with women and their horses, showing me that healing was never a one-way street. Just as he reflected my growth, I saw women in my clinics reflect their own transformations through their relationships with their horses. The ripple effect of his wisdom was undeniable. In the gentle guidance I gave or the quiet moments of trust between horse and rider, I saw RC's legacy come alive.

The Final Goodbye

In August 2021, I said goodbye to RC. He was just 13 years old, taken far too soon by a brain stem lesion that caused symptoms eerily reminiscent of Alzheimer's. Over the course of a year, I watched him slip away—some days present and connected, other days lost in a fog of fear and confusion.

Saying goodbye was one of the hardest things I've ever done. He was my partner, my teacher, my friend. I had imagined decades more with him, yet I was left with the heartbreak of an unfinished story. But RC's legacy didn't end with his passing. In the years since, his spirit has remained a constant presence, guiding me in ways I never expected.

Three years later, as I delved deeper into my own healing, RC surfaced in my vision—not as a memory but as a force, a reminder of everything he had taught me. He is gone in physical form, but his lessons, his love, and his light live on. I see his influence in every step I take to help others, and in every connection, I foster between women and their horses.

A Legacy of Freedom

RC's story is my story—a story that is one of heartbreak and healing, of stumbling and rising, of finding freedom in the most unexpected places. He taught me that freedom isn't about running away from fear but walking through it with courage and faith. He taught me that freedom isn't about running away from fear but walking through it with courage and faith. He showed me that healing is a journey of connection— between horse and human, between past and present, between who we are and who we are becoming.

The work I do today—helping women and their horses find trust, confidence, and connection—is RC's legacy as much as it is mine. Every retreat, every clinic, every moment spent bridging the gap between species carries his imprint. His lessons remind me to lead with love and authenticity, to share the treasures I found in the abyss, and to inspire others to step into their own freedom.

The Light That Remains

As I write these words, I can feel RC's presence—a golden light that warms my heart and steadies my spirit. His story is my story, a story that is one of heartbreak and healing, of stumbling and rising, of finding freedom in the most unexpected places.

RC is gone, but he is with me always. In every step I take, every connection I build, every life I touch, his legacy lives on. His lessons guide me as I continue to honor the bond we shared and the light he left behind.

And in that light, we are free.

Continue the Journey...

Breaking the Chains Within is more than a book—it's the beginning of a deeper path toward freedom, alignment, and embodied truth. If these pages stirred something in you—if you felt seen, moved, or awakened—you're not alone. And you don't have to walk this path by yourself.

I've created two powerful opportunities for women ready to continue this work in community, connection, and truth:

The Breaking the Chains Within Online Program

Join a growing circle of women walking this path together. This guided group coaching experience uses the book as our foundation for self-discovery, healing, and transformation. With live calls, reflection practices, and a supportive community space, this journey meets you where you are—and helps you grow from there.

The Breaking the Chains Within Retreats

Step into the pasture. Experience a week-long, in-person retreat with my herd and other like-minded women at the ranch. Here, we'll bring the teachings of the book to life in real time—through guided equine sessions, embodied coaching, and deeply grounded space for healing, truth, and reclamation.

You don't need to have it all figured out. You just need to say yes to what's calling you.

The Breaking the Chains Within approach is the heart of this work—carefully cultivated to guide women and horses into alignment, trust, and freedom. It's shared here for your personal journey. To teach, share, or build upon these principles professionally, please reach out to explore future trainings, licensing, or certification opportunities.

Stay connected. Get updates. And take the next step when you're ready.

→ Visit https://heartsoulhorsemanship.com/

→ Follow along on https://www.facebook.com/heartsoulconfidencebasedhorsemanship

→ Or email me directly at cyahart@yahoo.com

You've already begun the work. Now let's walk the rest of the way together.